47.95

D1172839

Group Counseling for Elementary and Middle School Children

Group Counseling for Elementary and Middle School Children

NINA W. BROWN

PRAEGER

Westport, Connecticut
London

Library of Congress Cataloging-in-Publication Data

Brown, Nina W.
　　Group counseling for elementary and middle school children / Nina
　　W. Brown.
　　　　p.　　cm.
　　Includes bibliographical references and index.
　　ISBN 0–275–94651–7
　　　　1. Counseling in elementary education—United States.　2. Group
　　counseling for children—United States.　I. Title.
　　LB1027.5.B77　　1994
　　372.14—dc20　　　　93–5396

British Library Cataloguing in Publication Data is available.

Library of Congress Catalog Card Number: 93–5396
ISBN: 0–275–94651–7

First published in 1994

Praeger Publishers, 88 Post Road West, Westport, CT 06881
An imprint of Greenwood Publishing Group, Inc.

Printed in the United States of America

The paper used in this book complies with the
Permanent Paper Standard issued by the National
Information Standards Organization (Z39.48–1984).

10 9 8 7 6 5 4 3 2 1

This book is dedicated to Billy and Joey,
The Emperors of the Universe

Contents

Preface

Counselors working in school settings with elementary and middle school children have a difficult job. Their work calls for a high level of preparation including education, self-understanding, sensitivity to others, and an awareness of the many life circumstances that impact the development of the child. They also face organizational demands not experienced by counselors in other settings and a set of expectations for accountability to the children, parents, teachers, directors of counseling, principals, and the community.

More and more school systems are mandating that the majority of the counselor's time be in either individual or group counseling. However, there are also constraints which help to work against the counselor, primarily that of time. Teachers want students to be helped, but are reluctant to release them from class because of the need for academic learning. They also do not want them to be out of class for several sessions. What usually happens is that the number of sessions for a child is restricted to 5 to 8 for the entire year. The counselor has to try to do a great deal in a short time.

This book was written to help counselors make effective and efficient use of whatever time is available by providing a framework for brief group counseling.

The underlying themes are that children can best be helped, in most instances, with group counseling, that group counseling can be preventive as well as remedial, and that the counselor is the vital component in making the group work and be productive. Also assumed is that there are limitations to group counseling and especially with brief groups. These limitations must be realized and accepted by the group leader if the most is to be made out of the time which is available.

While there are exercises and activities described in the book, a primary assumption is that they are to be adjunct to counseling, not the primary focus. The counselor should be careful not to overuse or overrely on them.

It is my hope that the book will prove useful and beneficial for children and to counselors.

Acknowledgments

I would like to thank everyone who helped me write this book. The clinicians who took the time and effort to publish their findings and experiences are too numerous to list, but their work significantly influenced mine. Not only do I thank them, but I would encourage others to emulate their example.

Carolyn Claude, my graduate assistant, deserves appreciation for the many hours of library work. Jean Lederle typed the manuscript and its changes cheerfully and deserves many thanks.

Finally, I would like to thank my husband Wilford for understanding my need for quiet in order to work.

Group Counseling for Elementary and Middle School Children

1

Introduction

OVERVIEW

This book concentrates on providing a conceptual framework for brief group counseling for elementary and middle school students. There are numerous books on counseling or therapy for this age group, but few address the underlying constraints and the impact on understanding of process, content, and the importance of the self of the group leader.

In addition to the conceptual framework, indirect methods for helping children access relevant material, develop awarenesses, and increase understanding of self and others are provided. All children are not verbally fluent, and even those who find it easier to express themselves with words may find it difficult to express complex thoughts and feelings. The indirect methods described give the leader additional resources to facilitate members' development.

Considerable attention is given to understanding and facilitating expressions of feelings and emotions. A distinction is made between the two for this book. Feelings are defined as simple expressions of affect and are commonly shared and understood experiences.

Emotions are thought to be more complex with the complexity deriving from the unique experiences of the person. For example, shaming experiences are not the same for all individuals, and that which causes one person to feel ashamed may not cause another to experience shame. Emotions have a learned component whereas feelings do not; they arise spontaneously within the individual.

Chapters 1 through 5 focus on basic definitions, presentation of theories and applications, Yalom's (1985) therapeutic factors adapted for this kind of group with children, the leader, the group, and group process. Chapters 6 and 7 discuss indirect techniques that use creative means to help understand underlying problems or concerns. Chapters 8 and 9 provide an expanded discussion and suggested strategies for dealing with feelings and emotions. Each chapter is briefly discussed.

Chapter 1 gives an overview for the book, basic assumptions about the makeup, constraints and possibilities for brief groups that are focused on in the book, types of therapeutic and therapy groups, negative coping strategies used by children, positive coping strategies used by children, and ethical and legal issues.

Chapter 2 presents major theories, applications, goals of therapy or counseling, and how group therapeutic factors can be used. Three levels for using theory, applications, and therapeutic factors are proposed and discussed. Level 1 focuses on symptom relief and prevention, Level 2 on education and learning new ways of communicating, relating, and so on, and Level 3 on deeper understanding and awarenesses. Conceptualization of counseling and therapy in this way provides an understanding of the possibilities and limitations of brief group counseling with this population. Suggestions for a hierarchical approach are also presented.

Chapter 3 discusses each of Yalom's therapeutic factors as it applies to brief group counseling for this setting and age group. The importance and relevance of each factor are presented as are some of the limitations. That is, some factors develop their therapeutic application over time and brief group counseling may be too short to make effective use of them.

Chapter 4 presents characteristics of the group leader and group dynamics. As it is essential that the leader be well prepared, considerable attention is given to this topic. Basic skills, awarenesses, and attitudes are discussed in relation to group process. It is assumed that knowledge of group dynamics and process contribute to successful outcomes, and thus the topic is discussed in some detail.

Chapter 5 discusses the pregroup planning process to include preparation of the leader, setting goals and objectives, choosing strategies, selection of group members, some administrative tasks that go along with the selection process, environmental concerns, pregroup interviews for members, structural concerns such as number and duration of sessions, and planning for evaluation.

Chapters 6 and 7 present indirect strategies that can facilitate group process. The emphasis is on expressive techniques such as art, imagery, drama fairy tales, and combinations of these techniques. Each is presented with a brief literature review, a discussion of applications and limitations, procedures for implementation, and suggested activities. The assumption underlying these chapters is that children may have difficulty adequately expressing complex thoughts or feelings, and that direct, verbal strategies are not always effective or efficient.

Chapters 8 and 9 focus on describing feelings and emotions, brief literature reviews, and suggestions for developing awareness of and working through these feelings and emotions. Chapter 8 highlights guilt, shame, and resentment and Chapter 9 focuses on anger, depression, and grief. Also included are discussions around some life circumstances that tend to produce these feelings and emotions such as divorce, death, temporary separations, and so on.

BASIC ASSUMPTIONS

Ideas presented in the book assume that there will be time-limited group sessions usually held in a school setting. Both the time available for sessions and the number of sessions will be brief. In many schools the only time available for students' participation in group sessions has to result in decreased classroom time. Time spent away from lessons is usually limited by the school no matter what the purpose may be. Because of these concerns and constraints, the underlying assumptions for group counseling described herein are that the number of sessions will be approximately 5 to 8 and the duration of each session will be 30 minutes for younger children to 50 minutes for older ones. It is a real challenge to devise and facilitate group therapy given these conditions.

These conditions dictate a high level of understanding and knowledge for the group leader. It is not enough to have 5 to 8 sessions of activities; the sessions must be planned, focused, and have therapeutic value. The leader needs to use considerable expertise to ensure that the sessions and the overall group are therapeutic in nature. Education, training, and self-understanding of the leader are crucial if these assumptions are to be met.

Basic education and training include the following: human growth and development with an emphasis on child development, sources of problems that lead to difficulties for children (e.g., familial, environmental, emotional, etc.), group theory and practice, intervention strategies, and psychopathology. Self-understanding of the group leader can be enhanced by having been a member of a personal growth or therapy group. Specific training as a group leader is essential and should include a supervised practicum or internship.

TYPES OF THERAPEUTIC AND THERAPY GROUPS

There are different types of groups and many try to classify them in various ways. Classification by Scheidlinger (1985) has four categories: group psychotherapy, therapeutic groups, human development and training groups, and self-help groups. Gazda (1989) also has four categories: group guidance, group counseling, group psychotherapy, and self-help. Corey (1990) lists group psychotherapy, structured groups, group counseling, and self-help groups. All appear to have some commonalities even though the terminology differs.

Scheidlinger (1985) describes group psychotherapy as using a psychosocial process with a focus on emotional interactions. These groups are led by a trained clinician and have members who can be characterized as having personality or interpersonal dysfunction.

Therapeutic groups are all other groups, according to Scheidlinger. They are considered to be auxiliary or in conjunction with the primary mode of treatment and do not stand on their own. They are focused on remediation or to develop optimal functioning. Examples of therapeutic groups are art, movement, and so forth.

Human development and training groups are affectively and cognitively focused. The leaders are mental health educators and group members are not considered to be seriously disturbed.

Self-help groups are composed of members who have shared common problems or needs. They may or may not have a professional leader. The focus is on providing emotional support.

Gazda (1989) proposes a model of groups that has overlapping goals and professional competencies for the leader. Group guidance has goals of developing coping and social skills that are designed to prevent development of problems. It can continue across the life span and is not limited to one setting or age group. Group counseling is also preventive and growth enhancing. However, there is some remediation involved. Sensitivity groups, T-groups, organizational groups, encounter groups, and structured groups fall into this category. Psychotherapy groups have the focus of remediation and members tend to be moderately to severely dysfunctional. Self-help groups are defined as those whose members have common problems/concerns and who meet to provide emotional support for each other, with or without a leader.

Corey (1990) describes group counseling as focusing on "growth, development, enhancement, prevention, self-awareness, and releasing blocks to growth" (p.11). He describes group psychotherapy as having a focus on remediation, treatment, and personality reconstruction. Structured groups are short-term groups that deal with a theme and a specific population, such as adult children of alcoholics. He considers self-help groups to give support to members who have a common problem where the group helps them cope with psychological stress.

There are more commonalities than differences in the various descriptions and definitions of groups. For example, all definitions of self-help groups emphasize that they are voluntary, formed around common problems or handicaps, emphasize face-to-face interactions, the role of a mental health professional is minimized or absent, and they provide emotional support. Psychotherapy groups are perceived as problem-focused with an emphasis on remediation or repair of injury or deficit. Group counseling falls somewhere in between these two depending on needs of group members and goals for the group.

The kind of group described in this book proposes that some portion of all three is useful in brief groups for children. The understandings of psychic development, transference, projection, projective identification, and countertransference from psychotherapy; use of prevention and personal growth as an emphasis from counseling, and the self-help group's focus on encouraging emotional support among members and development of more effective coping strategies.

Brief groups in the book are also more theme-oriented than problem-focused. While group members may have shared concerns or problems, the commonalities are more on the order of underlying issues than common situations. For example, the underlying issue may be loss for all group members, but the situations of loss for each may not be the same. Some may have experienced a death in the family, others divorce, but the common theme is loss. In other words, the group leader does not have to create groups composed of members who have the same experiences that are problematic to them. Group members can be selected on the basis of shared themes.

NEGATIVE COPING STRATEGIES

Brenner (1984) proposes four broad categories of evasive coping strategies used by children: denial, regression, withdrawal, and impulsive acting out. All have the goal of keeping anxiety at bay and, even if effective in the short term, have negative effects in the long term. If anxiety is recognized and dealt with rather than evaded, there are more positive outcomes for healthy development.

Denial is a defense mechanism whereby one simply refuses to recognize or accept the existence of anxiety around a person, situation, or event. The Dictionary of Psychotherapy says that denial is "commonly associated with splitting and is therefore to be included amongst the primitive defense mechanisms" (p. 93). Melanie Klein (St. Clair, 1986) defined splitting as separating or keeping apart feelings and aspects of self. The infant uses splitting to protect him/herself by disbursing dangerous feelings and keeping them away from gratifying feelings. When splitting persists and the split-off part is not accepted or integrated then more troubling conditions can develop, such as borderline and narcissistic disorders (Mahler, 1968; Kernberg, 1990).

Regression to an earlier state and becoming more dependent and demanding is a coping strategy that can produce a positive payoff for the child. Payoffs could be receiving more physical contact, such as hugs, or more nurturing. Some regression can be tolerated for a short period if adults understand the reason for the regression and take positive steps to help the child work through feelings around the situation that caused them to resort to regressive behaviors. If these behaviors persist then more intensive therapy may be indicated.

Withdrawal can be either physical, psychological or both. It is the child's way of running away from anxiety. They may concentrate their time and energy on things, excessive daydreams, pets, and so on, anything to keep from interacting with others in any significant way. When the strategy works to relieve tension, it may increase and will most certainly persist. Some negative outcomes for persistent withdrawal behavior are increased loneliness and isolation, social immaturity, and an inability to develop an emotional support system.

Impulsive acting out is a way of not dealing with anxiety around past events that produced the anxiety as they are busy doing something that provokes others and/or are dealing with the result of their acting out. These behaviors are most often noticed as they call for a reaction from others. In contrast, denial, regression, and withdrawal are internal states that may or may not be noticed by others. Impulsive acting-out behaviors turn into self-destructive behaviors in the long run.

POSITIVE COPING STRATEGIES

Brenner (1984) also lists five positive ways that children use to cope: altruism, humor, suppression, anticipation, and sublimination. These are primarily positive but they can also have negative aspects. An adult has to be alert to the possibility that, when these strategies are used over time, they may come to mask real feelings which are not being acknowledged.

Altruism, used this way, means that you help yourself by helping others. The child may avoid dealing with his/her own anxiety by being helpful to parents, siblings, teachers, and so forth. Because they are giving of themselves to others, it is usually perceived as very positive and is praised and rewarded. However, when a child assumes the role of taking care of others, he/she gives up some childhood roles such as being carefree and irresponsible. This kind of altruistic behavior persisting into adulthood can result in the individual putting everyone's needs ahead of his/her own.

Humor is used to express anger and pain. Sarcastic remarks, teasing, and acting the clown are humor strategies to cope with anxiety. Instead of crying and asking for help openly, they keep others at a distance with their humor. Others may laugh at and with them, but they don't understand the use to which humor is being put.

Suppression of painful feelings can be very useful. It enables one to put aside the pain for a little while and to concentrate on something else that is more positive. For example, children who are experiencing grief because of a death in the family will suppress their sadness and engage in play for a period of time. They will laugh, run around, and have fun. Then, they return to the sorrowful feelings. Suppression, however, when used to excess can become denial.

Anticipation is used by children who have faced several stressors or painful events. They begin to plan for the next event while experiencing this one. By concentrating on planning, they avoid having to deal with the present one. Children of alcoholics, those who are abused, and those who have faced several losses may cope by anticipating the next event. The negative side is that they never learn to deal with the here and now and may become so fearful of what lies ahead that they are reluctant to do anything that isn't planned for in advance. These children lose spontaneity.

Games, hobbies, sports, clubs, and so on are examples of how sublimination is used to cope with anxiety. While not all children participating in these are using them to sublimate anxiety, some are. A negative consequence of sublimination is withdrawal from others who are facing the same situation producing the anxiety, for example, other family members.

ETHICAL AND LEGAL ISSUES

All group leaders should be familiar with the ethical guidelines or their professional organization, licensing or accrediting board, and with the legal expectations of the organization or group with which they work. Most all professional mental health groups have specific ethical guidelines for group leaders. These guidelines emphasize adequacy of education and training, protection of individuals, informed consent, and confidentiality.

Many school systems have specific requirements that dictate how ethical and legal issues are to be handled. For example, parental permission is usually required before a child can participate in group counseling. Both the child and his/her parents should know and understand the purpose of the group and expected achievements.

There will usually be specific requirements dictating what must be reported to the authorities or supervisor. Most school systems require that suspected or reported child abuse be brought to the attention of the principal. Under these conditions, confidentiality cannot be ensured or adhered to consistently. For these and other reasons, it is essential that the counselor be aware of legal restraints before leading groups.

It is difficult to accept that confidentiality cannot be maintained and because it cannot, safety in the group is affected. There are reasons other than legal constraints why confidentiality cannot be ensured. The group leader cannot guarantee that members will not disclose confidential material outside the group setting. The need for confidentiality should and can be emphasized, but it cannot be guaranteed.

2

A Conceptualization of Theory, Application, and Therapeutic Factors

Theory is fundamental to counseling and therapy. It provides the foundation and framework for much of what the therapist does, and for expected outcomes. The theoretical stance of the therapist determines what assumptions are held about how humans grow and develop physically, cognitively, and psychologically, goals of therapy, responsibilities and actions of the therapist, assumptions about the client's problem/concern, and techniques to be used.

Many counselors and therapists term themselves eclectic because they may not have found any one theory that explains enough for them, or because they like to use techniques from many different theories. Even in these cases, the therapist is operating from a particular theoretical base including the philosophical assumptions underlying the theory. However, if one is not firmly grounded in and aware of his/her basic theoretical foundation, therapy is apt to be less effective as techniques are being used without an adequate rationale or expected outcome.

An examination of practices by therapists would probably show that most freely borrow techniques associated with theories other than the one with which they were educated to use, or the one that is their preference. For example, many classically trained psycho-therapists use cognitive techniques, and an existential therapist will use contracting with clients. However, most of their therapeutic interventions conform to the expectations embedded in their theoretical orientation.

Being firmly grounded in theory is essential for those therapists having to practice brief counseling and is crucial for effective brief counseling with children. There is not enough time to explore, allow issues to emerge, or to practice new behaviors until they are internalized. However, merely dealing with symptoms is not all that can be accomplished if the therapist is knowledgeable. It may be even more important for those engaging in brief counseling to have a deeper understanding so as to select interventions that have a high probability of quick success.

The following discussion proposes a three-level approach to conceptualizing theory, applications, and use of group therapeutic factors. Brief group therapy can use the first two levels but extensive time is needed to engage in Level 3 therapy. However, therapists and counselors need the understandings embedded in theories associated with Level 3 and, while using concepts from theories in Levels 1 and 2, may conduct therapy from the basis in Level 3. Further, seeds can be planted that would encourage clients to seek the deeper awarenesses and understandings that can occur with longer-term group therapy.

The following discussions are not intended to be a description of theories. The reader is encouraged to read basic books on each theory for a better understanding as space does not permit an adequate presentation nor is it the focus of this book. What will be presented are some of the concepts and techniques associated with the theory that have application to brief group counseling with elementary and middle school students.

LEVELS FOR COUNSELING AND THERAPY

Table 2.1 presents a summary of therapeutic goals for each level, major theories that have applications, and therapeutic factors that are more easily used at that level. While it is possible to use all

Table 2.1
Levels of Goals, Factors, and Theories

Major Therapeutic Goals	Major Group Therapeutic Factors	Major Theories
LEVEL 1		
Symptom relief	Universality	Behavioral
Establish relationship	Instill hope	Rational-Emotive
Promote safety	Guidance	Person-centered
Clarify goals	Altruism	Group-as-a-whole
LEVEL 2		
Learn new ways to relate to others	Interpersonal learning	Person-centered
Learn new ways to communicate	Group cohesion	Transactional Analysis
Learn how others perceive you	Learning social-ization skills	Psychodrama
Develop an awareness of unfinished business or unresolved issues		Gestalt Group-as-a-whole
LEVEL 3		
Develop an under-standing of influences of the past on present functioning	Family reenactment	Psychodynamic Existential Group-as-a-whole
Develop effective ways of relating, functioning	Catharis	Object-relations
Develop open expression of feelings	Existential factors	Self-psychology
Heightened sense of self	Self-understanding	Person-centered

therapeutic factors at each level, some will probably need more time to be fully effective or experienced in the group.

The levels also follow the stages of group development in some ways and may be hierarchical in nature. That is, one level must be established before the next can be effectively addressed.

Although theories are assigned to different levels, these are not fixed. Some theories can be effectively used at more than one level but appear to have more direct application to the suggested level. For example, Behavioral theory can be directly applied to symptom relief which is at Level 1. It can also be used to produce new learning which is on Level 2. It is more difficult to see its application to Level 3 which emphasizes understanding, as the theory's foundation is not based on the individual's understanding self. On the other hand, psychodynamic theory is considered to be long term, and focused on the individual coming to understand how he/she developed psychologically. Thus, it is difficult to use this theory for symptom relief which is a more short-term goal. Of course, it is desirable that the symptom relief be long term, but many need the short-term relief.

Some theories that will be discussed transcend the levels. That is, they function in some ways at each level. Theories falling into this category are Person-centered, Group-as-a-whole, and Existential.

Person-centered theory has been found to be important in helping to develop a therapeutic relationship. It emphasizes characteristics and skills that convey the therapist's caring and valuing of the client(s). The characteristics of genuineness, acceptance, positive regard, caring, warmth, and understanding of the inner world of the other have been found to be basic, whatever theoretical approach is used. Skills of attending, active listening and responding, clarifying, and confronting are also used in most theories when applied in therapy. Numerous studies have documented that these are critical in developing a therapeutic relationship.

Group-as-a-whole theories can also transcend levels. These theories emphasize using the resources of the group to help individuals rather than working with individuals in a group setting. While individual concerns/problems/issues are addressed in this theory, the process for doing so is different. These theories assume that all members in the group have the capacity and potential for helping other members and that it is not solely the responsibility of the leader. Other characteristics of these theories include focusing on systems; understanding dynamics of the group, not always just the dynamics of the individual; and using interventions that highlight how the group process is reflective of the individual.

Existential theory transcends all levels as it is based on a philosophy which determines how individuals are perceived, the environment and limitations of both. These theories are very useful in helping the therapist understand and use the human condition for therapeutic purposes. Yalom (1985) notes that existential factors appear to be present in all therapy groups regardless of theoretical orientation, group focus, or goals of therapy. Even when the primary goal is short-term symptom relief, these factors emerge, although they may not be dealt with or even recognized at the time.

LEVEL 1

Major Therapeutic Goals

The overriding desire for most who come to group therapy is to feel better, have better relationships, to understand self and others, and/or to have a more fulfilling life. Members of therapy groups, even seemingly homogenous groups, have very different goals for therapy. Many adult members cannot articulate their goals, some are not aware of their real goals and, in addition to all of these, children don't always understand the possibilities that are open to them and may have unrealistic goals. However, for many group members the primary goal is relief of symptoms. They are uncomfortable, anxious, have debilitating psychological pain, inadequate relationships, and so on. What they desire most is relief from these conditions as soon as possible. They may not be interested in antecedents of the conditions or understandings, they want to feel better, NOW.

Establishing a therapeutic relationship consists of building trust between the therapist and client, helping the client develop a sense of safety, ensuring that the client feels accepted and cared for as a worthwhile unique individual, communicating understanding, and creating a climate where thoughts and feelings can be expressed openly and freely. A therapeutic relationship is basic to effective therapy and not much therapy takes place until it is established.

Group members have to feel safe before relevant self-disclosure occurs. Feelings of safety are not the same for all members of the group. Indeed, many cannot tell you what makes them feel safe or unsafe in the group. This is a process that must occur over time, as many who come to group have been betrayed, abandoned or disappointed in the past to the extent that it is difficult for them to trust anyone enough to feel safe. Creating a group climate that promotes safety and meets those diverse needs must be attended to when the group is in the planning stage. The chapter on Creation of the Group addresses this issue in more detail.

Members come to the group most often with unclear goals. They are unsure what they want to accomplish for themselves (except for desiring symptom relief) and have little or no concept of what they want from the group. The leader can help immensely by helping members to clarify their goals for themselves and for the group. Once members understand where they want to go, it is easier to help them get there.

Major Therapeutic Factors

Chapter 3 provides definitions, describes the importance of factors in group process, and illustrates techniques to establish therapeutic factors. The discussion in this section will be limited to pointing out the usefulness at each level.

Universality helps members feel less alone. It is important for the group leader to help members understand their similarities, for this is how they begin to see that they are not the only ones with this problem/issue/concern or situation. While no two are exactly the same, enough communalities exist so that members can identify with each other.

Hopelessness is incapacitating. When members cannot see any way out of their dilemma or situation they suffer a form of paralysis.

Therefore, one of the first tasks of the group leaders is to help group members realize that they can get better, or cope more effectively. It is only when one is hopeful that the real work can begin, for that is when the client becomes an active participant in the process. Belief in their capacity to function more effectively, to relate better to others, that the therapist can guide them out of this dilemma, and that the process of therapy is beneficial all contribute to positive outcomes for group members. The importance of hope for the client cannot be underestimated.

Guidance provides correct information to clear up misperceptions or misunderstandings about processes, procedures, growth, and development. In short, guidance deals with factual data to help the person become more fully informed. It is not advice giving, but it does focus on gaps in knowledge or misinformation the person might have.

Children can benefit from guidance in many ways. Being knowledgeable gives them a sense of confidence that they can navigate and compete successfully in the world. They realize that they have more alternatives from which to choose, and they get support for making decisions. All of this can take place in the relative safety of the group.

Altruism refers to helping others. Children are usually in the position of receiving help and they are seldom made aware that they have something of value to give to others. The group setting can provide opportunities for them to become aware of what they can do to help others, what others feel they have that is valuable, and the sense that they can contribute to the growth and welfare of others. Even when children need considerable help they also have something to give to others. Group leaders can use this therapeutic factor to help both individuals and the group.

Major Theories

The discussion that follows focuses on the primary applications of theories to Level 1 brief group counseling with elementary and middle school children. The summaries are intended to provide an overview of major concepts that have direct utility but are not all inclusive. For a more in-depth understanding of theories, it is suggested that the reader consult original sources or texts that have theories as their primary topic.

Rational-Emotive Therapy (RET). RET was chosen to discuss as an example of the cognitive-behavioral approach. RET was developed by Albert Ellis (1992) who postulates that people disturb themselves rather than being disturbed by outside influences. The goal of therapy is to undo irrational thinking and to initiate more constructive behaviors.

RET techniques specifically useful for group counseling include forceful coping self-statements, rational emotive imagery, shame-attacking exercises, role-playing, stories, fables and analogies, and humor.

Behaviorally oriented techniques usually combined with cognitive approaches include desensitization, reinforcement and penalties, response prevention, relapse prevention, and skill training.

Using RET in group counseling, interventions take place with individual members in the group setting. The leader addresses each member in turn, focusing on his/her homework. The member relates progress, lack of progress, presenting new problems or returning to old ones. Interactions between members and developing a therapeutic relationship are not emphasized. The primary work is done between leader and member.

Although many of the techniques used in RET are applicable in the first stage of the model, these are not the primary reason for applying RET here. RET is more useful because it assumes that changing thinking will change behavior. Changes in thinking and behavior can also bring symptom relief as well as new ways of behaving. Helping children to understand that they have the power to construct their view of themselves and teaching them how to keep from incorporating views of others that negatively impact them is very important in instilling hope that they can get or feel better. Techniques such as bibliotherapy, role-playing, stories or fables, and so on are very useful in short-term group counseling with children.

Behavioral. The many contributions of Behavioral therapy with children are well known. It is especially useful at the first level in the model because specific behaviors can be focused on and techniques applied that help to change these behaviors. Many times behaviors are reflective of symptoms, and changing behavior can result in symptom relief.

In the Behavioral approach the therapist is not interested in the client's past, unconscious material, or other internal states. It is focused on specified behavior which is also considered to be the problem. The literature suggests that having a narrow focus like this can produce change in a fairly short time. Using reinforcement, contingency management techniques, and flooding have all been shown to be effective. The primary techniques used are all based on theories of learning.

Uses of Behavioral theory in brief group counseling with children include focusing on specific behaviors, specifying goals of treatment, setting up a plan of action, reinforcing the behavior that one wishes to continue, and developing a plan to extinguish undesired behaviors. Children get a sense that things can get better soon, that they play a part in their getting better, and can feel structure that may be lacking in other parts of their lives.

Person-Centered. Building a therapeutic relationship is usually considered to be essential in most theoretical approaches to therapy. The relationship is important in group counseling, for it allows trust to develop between members and between members and leader, thus fostering group cohesion and self-disclosure.

Rogers (1975) developed the theory which proposes that group members have the potential for self-direction rather than the group leader leading or directing them where to go. He also proposed that the selfhood of the therapist was a crucial factor. That is, the self-awareness, self-understanding, and inner acceptance of self all contribute to the ability of the therapist to sense and understand the inner world of the other person. The therapist's selfhood allows the therapeutic relationship to develop.

The therapist must communicate to the client(s) genuineness, warmth, caring, acceptance, respect, nonjudgmental positive regard, and empathy. Techniques used to accomplish this are active listening, reflection, clarification, and an understanding of the inner world of the client.

This theory proposes that a great deal of self-work be done before becoming a therapist; it cuts across other theories and certainly is applicable across all levels in the model. It more clearly defines what characteristics are expected of the therapist and identifies basic counseling skills.

Group-As-A-Whole. The Group-as-a-whole theory assumes a systems approach to group therapy. That is, there are individuals in the group whose needs must be addressed but the basic unit in the group is subgroups and not individuals (Agazarian, 1992). The group itself is also an entity and individuals are helped through use of the group as an entity and by dealing with the system.

The dynamics in the group are constantly shifting and changing as are the subgroups. Agazarian (1992) proposes that "members sub-group around similarities and dissolve around differences." One of the leader's tasks is to help members identify similarities and differences. This is not an easy task, as apparent similarities contain differences and apparent differences contain similarities. Focusing on similarities or differences at times helps group members to perceive the therapeutic factor of universality or come to grips with the existential awareness of their aloneness in the universe.

There are times when what is occurring in the group is a reflection of what is happening with individuals in the group. For example, the group is stalled because anger is not being expressed directly. This may also be a reflection of individual members' reluctance to own and express their own anger directly. Learning to tune in to the group as a whole is useful in many ways for using the resources of the group to enhance the ability to help individuals in the group.

The group leader must become adept at helping members identify similarities and differences. But it is not enough to merely identify them. The similarities or differences must be clarified and expanded upon. Members need to become more adept at identifying similarities and differences and understanding the significance of them for their issues/concerns/problems.

EDUCATION AND UNDERSTANDING LEVELS

While education and learning can occur at any level and neither symptom relief nor establishing a therapeutic relationship is necessary for learning to occur, it is placed on Level 2 in this model on the premise that more learning and deeper learning take place after the tasks of Level 1 have been accomplished. Trust, hope, appreciation of universality, meeting safety needs, and some symptom relief allow group members to begin to explore themselves and to engage in meaningful self-disclosure.

The model also assumes that understanding develops over time and that successful completion of most of the tasks on Levels 1 and 2 contribute to understanding self and how it came to be. This deeper understanding is unlikely to be accomplished in brief group therapy which is limited, by definition, to five to eight sessions. However, if members participate in a series of these brief sessions it is possible to begin to address some of the deeper understandings. Another possibility is that seeds are planted at the earlier levels; seeds that will create in the individual an interest to know and understand more and make him/her want to go deeper. These individuals may voluntarily seek out the kind of group therapy that leads to this level of self-understanding.

LEVEL 2

Major Therapeutic Goals

The second level can be defined as one of expanding awarenesses and learning at a deeper level—not just learning for symptom relief, but learning over a broad spectrum that can result in new ways of communicating and relating to others, becoming aware of how the past is influencing present behavior, and learning expanded ways to express feelings appropriately. The client turns from a solely personal focus to incorporate an awareness of his/her impact on others and, in doing so, becomes open to learning more effective ways of interacting with others.

A broader and deeper awareness of self, personal issues, and desired outcomes also accompanies the turning inward. By understanding self better, individuals can become better able to understand and relate to others. The two complement each other. Whereas much of the focus on Level 1 is personal or inward, Level 2 can incorporate both.

The Johari window concept (Johnson and Johnson, 1975) illustrates a part of this. It proposes that there are four parts to "self": the part known to you and also seen by others, the part known to you but kept hidden from others, the part seen by others but not seen by you, and the part hidden from you and from others. As you begin to explore your self you expand the known parts and decrease the hidden parts. Group counseling facilitates the knowing of self both for you and for others.

Accepting that there are parts of self that are hidden from you and having the desire to know these parts better begin the process. Parts of self that are hidden may even have been known to you at one time and need to be rediscovered. While it may be somewhat difficult to accept that there are parts of self that are seen by others but hidden from you, becoming aware of how you are perceived by others adds to learning. This is particularly useful when there is group consensus to validate the perception. When you become aware that other group members are in agreement, it becomes easier to accept that what others are perceiving is a part of you of which you were not aware.

The group plays an important role in discovering hidden parts of self. Other members start out by seeing you as you present yourself, influenced in part by their perceptual veil. As the group process unfolds, they become aware of your projections, transferences, and defenses that help keep parts of self hidden. Members can make these visible to each other by pointing them out directly. As awareness expands, so do the hidden parts of self. One of the outcomes of increasing the known parts of self and decreasing the hidden parts, according to the theory, is that one is then better able to relate to others in satisfying ways. Another way of saying this is that the more open and accepting of self you are, the more you are able to be open to and accepting of others.

The group leader can help provide many opportunities for learning on Level 2. Goals and objectives for the group and for sessions can be formulated so as to increase learning. Strategies used can be designed to target needed development. The suggested theories applied to Level 2 all have a focus on learning more about self and how one relates to others.

Major Theories

Theories associated with Level 2 have some commonalities. They are all active theories, that is, the group facilitator does something more than just allowing the process to emerge and learning to take place. All also assume that the therapeutic relationship is important to the process and they have a strong educational component. The following discussion focuses on three theories, Gestalt, Transactional Analysis, and Psychodrama. Person-centered, Group-as-a-whole, and Existential are also relevant for this level but are not discussed here.

Gestalt. Gestalt theory is particularly useful for group counseling with children because it assumes that the here and now experience is the most important. Children don't have to try to recall past events because present experiencing can be used to understand the past and its impact. Further, the group leader focuses on how and what, not why. This focus prevents any potential misunderstanding that blame or criticism is attached.

Techniques associated with Gestalt therapy are very action-oriented with a lot of attention given to physical or nonverbal responses. The group leader helps members to become aware of how they are blocking energy and expressing resistance by focusing on bodily sensations. Other action-oriented techniques include assuming both sides in a conflict and speaking for both, or becoming aware of the conflicted "self" and speaking for both sides of the conflicted self.

The group leader is guided by certain assumptions of the theory: that people are personally responsible for what they feel, that they must take responsibility for their feelings, and that ultimately they must take responsibility for providing their own support. In short, while others are important, the ultimate responsibility for how you are, how you function and how you feel is yours. Others have an impact but you have the power to decide who and what you will be.

A group leader using Gestalt theory would make sure the following items were part of the group process:

a. A here-and-now focus versus a there-and-then.

b. Not only bringing the past into the present but also bringing the future into the present.

c. Detecting patterns of accepting and avoiding responsibility for group members and making them aware of these patterns.

d. Identifying unfinished business that is impacting present behavior, such as guilt, unexpressed resentment, interrupted or unexpressed grief.

e. Developing an awareness of how language is used. For example, expressing "shoulds," "oughts," a reliance on qualifiers, e.g. maybe, sort of, etc., not making "I" statements.

f. Increasing awareness of bodily sensations and their meanings.

Transactional Analysis. Transactional Analysis (TA) is easily applied to group therapy in Level 2 because its goals and objectives focus on teaching members how they interact with others, how early decisions are still influencing them, how to become aware of the games they play and the scripts they live out. Therapists and counselors are seen primarily as teachers. They teach awareness, new ways of behaving and relating.

Group members learn what ego states are, injunctions or messages that have been incorporated into their life styles, and scripts that structure their lives. They become more aware of how they may be seeking out situations to keep the bad feelings alive in order to justify their life scripts.

Transactional Analysis refers to interpreting communication patterns with emphasis on increasing awareness of which ego state is operating when interacting with others. Structural analysis seeks to help individuals understand their life script and what decisions and when early decisions were made. Game analysis focuses on identifying defense and other mechanisms used to accomplish hidden agendas and protect against intimacy. Once transactions, life scripts, and games are better understood, the individual can make a conscious decision to change.

Some specific techniques of TA lend themselves to use with children in groups. Contracting sets parameters, defines expectations, encourages acceptance of personal responsibility, and provides a measure of accomplishment. Contracts are set by group members together with the leader and are intended to reflect what they want to change, what they will do to promote change, and how they will behave in the group. The group leader is expected to facilitate fulfilling contracts for group members.

The primary tool used is teaching: teaching what ego states are, how to recognize which ego state is present in communications, defining personal life positions, and defining steps, strategies, and techniques for positive change.

Psychodrama. Psychodrama is one of the few theories developed specifically for group therapy. Developed by J. L. Moreno to help patients achieve catharsis and thereby achieve deeper understanding and integration, it is an action-oriented approach to achieve goals based on psychoanalytic principles.

The psychodramatic group uses drama techniques to experience or act out situations from the past, present, or future. Members role play to express feelings, get in touch with unrecognized or unrealized parts of self, act out conflicts or crises, test reality, and to develop spontaneity and creativity.

A psychodrama has a stage, a director, a protagonist, auxiliary egos, and an audience. The stage is where the action takes place and is representing the life space of the member performing. The protagonist is the person performing the psychodrama of his/her personal life situation. The group leader is the director and has the responsibilities of planning the session, warming up the group, and leading the summary discussion.

Each group member becomes a protagonist who then acts out a scene or scenes from an important event or situation. The acting is present-centered and persons from the past are brought into the scene and interacted with as if they were present. The protagonist usually selects other group members to act as auxiliary egos. Protagonists prepare auxiliary egos to act their parts by describing the person on whom the role is modeled.

Auxiliary egos may portray significant people in the life of the protagonist or any emotionally-laden object or thing, such as a pet. They may also verbalize the feelings and emotions of the protagonist that they perceive as important but are being ignored or suppressed.

The audience observes and gives feedback during the discussion phase. They are encouraged to identify with the protagonist and, in so doing, work on their personal issues.

There are three phases of a psychodrama, warm-up, action and discussion. The session is begun by having members identify and discuss briefly any relationships, conflicts, etc. that are significant for them that they would like to explore through psychodrama. The action phase involves the acting out by the protagonist and auxiliary egos. The group leader facilitates discussion about the experience. Many of the concepts and procedures used in psychodrama were adapted for use in the drama techniques for children groups described in Chapter 7.

LEVEL 3

The most important point about Level 3 is that achievement on this level is a prerequisite for group leaders. That is, the groups they lead may not operate on this level, but the understanding of the emotional, psychological, and cognitive development of group members by the leader is necessary if effective interventions are to be made.

Major Therapeutic Goals

Level 3 therapeutic goals are those that are usually developed over time with guidance. Some degree of accomplishment is possible on the other levels, but a deep understanding and self-actualization are realized only after much self-exploration.

Understanding how the past is influencing present functioning begins with identifying what events, people, situations, and so forth in the past are connected. While all may be important, some are more significant than others. Children, in particular, have little understanding of the impact of these factors on their development. It is more important for the group leader to understand so as to make appropriate intervention(s) than it is to have the child understand.

Some maturity appears to facilitate understanding of the past and its impact.

Developing self-understanding to the degree that one becomes more effective in relating to others, developing and maintaining meaningful relationships, and becoming more self-actualized is a process that can best be accomplished over time. It is unlikely that this can be accomplished in brief (5–8 sessions) group counseling. It may be possible to make progress toward these goals if sets of group counseling are used, that is, the person participates in several sets of five to eight sessions over time. Unless this is planned for at the beginning of counseling for the individual and sets are designed to build one on the other, he/she most likely will not be able to achieve this degree of self-understanding.

Major Theories

Psychoanalytic. Psychoanalytic theory assumes that personality is determined by unconscious motivations, early childhood experiences, and sexual and aggressive forces. Uncovering the unconscious and making it conscious is basic to understanding the individual. Thus, much of the work done by the counselor focuses on understanding the early years for their impact on personality and behavior. Resolving conflicts at different stages of psychosexual development is a key part of therapy.

Group sessions allow the re-creation of the family and original dynamics present in the family. Group members are related to in terms of transferences from the family and other important individuals. Learning the transferences and their antecedents is helpful to the individual in resolving old conflicts that may be unconsciously impacting present behavior and relationships.

Even in brief group counseling the understanding and use of transference, resistance, and defense mechanisms can play an important role. There isn't enough time to develop the kind of therapeutic relationship that will allow the acceptance of interpretations that focus on early relationships and experiences, but the leader's understanding of how these are manifested in the group can be fruitful cues for interventions. They don't have to be labelled, accepted, and worked through, necessarily; the leader can just note them, call them to the attention of the member, and suggest other ways of responding, relating, or behaving. A deeper understanding by the group member needs time to develop.

Some techniques used in Psychoanalytic therapy that may be useful in brief group counseling with children are free association, dream analysis, and freedom to express any thought, fantasy or desire.

Object-relations. Object-relations theory can be thought of as a subset of Psychoanalytic theory. Instead of focusing on uncovering the unconscious or psychosexual development, Object-relations theory seeks to understand the psychic development of the child and to repair trauma or injury. It assumes that the self develops from real or fantasized interrelationships starting in infancy.

Object-relations theorists focus on primitive defense mechanisms such as splitting, projective identification, omnipotent denials, projection, and introjection—mental representations of others that trigger behavioral responses and interchanges taking place between the self and internal images of others or mental residues of their relations with the self (Ganzarain, 1992).

Group therapy allows early developmental traumas or injuries to be repaired through the group assumption of the surrogate "good mothering" role and as a container for negative emotions without retaliation. Modeling how to deal with negative influences, anxieties, and defense mechanisms is facilitated in the group setting.

The group leader can best use this theory in an attempt to understand how the individual came to be. Accepting that the group provides an opportunity to be a surrogate good-enough mother, and the container for negative emotions provides an environment where much self-learning and understanding can result even in brief counseling.

Self-psychology. Self-psychology (Kohut, 1971) theory proposes that empathic failures (particularly in early life) of the self-object lead to narcissistic injuries that evoke anxiety. The empathic failures result from either underresponsiveness or overresponsiveness by the self-object. Self-object is an external "object" that provides the appropriate "self" and over whom one has control. In essence, the child then experiences a loss of control over the "self," which results in injury. Counseling and therapy begin with trying to understand the world of the client empathically.

While the emphasis on empathically understanding the other is similar to that proposed by Person-centered theory, there are significant differences. Whereas in Person-centered therapy empathy is used to convey to the other that he/she is understood and valued, in Self-psychology empathy is used for understanding and to repair injury. Person-centered therapy is nondirective while self-psychology tends to be more directive, although not as directive as Psychoanalytic therapy.

3

Yalom's Therapeutic Factors in Brief Groups for Children

Most of Yalom's 11 therapeutic factors are self-explanatory and data are available that suggest their usefulness. However, most studies have focused on adult psychiatric patients and little has been done to establish empirical evidence for children. It is perhaps even more crucial to understand basic therapeutic factors in brief group counseling for children than it is for longer-term group therapy with adults. The constraints of time and the lesser ability of children to adequately communicate using words make group work more difficult.

The following discussion of therapeutic factors is intended to highlight their importance, recognition, and strategies to promote their development. It should be remembered that few groups in school settings will have more than five to eight sessions. Proper planning can ensure constructive outcomes, but tapping into and using therapeutic factors can make the experience even more rewarding and meaningful.

YALOM'S THERAPEUTIC FACTORS

Yalom's (1985) therapeutic factors are described in the following discussion. Also discussed are suggested applications for use with children in brief group counseling.

Instillation of Hope

Group members need to believe that they will get better (i.e., hurt less or not hurt at all). Members need to believe that counseling and the leader will be effective. This is more difficult to accomplish in brief therapy because the barriers to installation of hope, the establishing of relationships, working through resistances, understanding transferences, projections, and projective identifications, identifying and lowering of defenses all take time to accomplish.

Working with children in school settings may have the disadvantage of having only a few group sessions (5–8), but there is also an advantage, that of having the same child, or children, in several groups over the years they spend in the school. Thus, installation of hope can begin in the first group and has the potential of being developed more fully over time. Further, mixing children in a group who are at different levels in internalizing this therapeutic factor expands the number of individuals in the group from whom others may learn how to hope.

Strategies to develop this therapeutic factor include establishing a relationship with each member that will allow trust to develop, planning sessions to accomplish a therapeutic goal, not merely having activities or a series of activities, and trying to ensure that there are other group members who can model hope.

Universality

Children, like adults, need to know that their situation, feelings, and so on are shared by others. This therapeutic factor reduces the sense of isolation, feelings of being strange or weird, and can aid in reduction of shame. By recognizing that one is not the only person in the world to have this kind of experience (the assumption is that no two experiences are exactly the same), connectedness to others is fostered and the notion that one is forever flawed is attacked.

Shame develops when one feels there is an inherent flaw over which one has no control and the flaw can never be overcome. Shame also prevents one from revealing relevant information from a fear of also revealing this fatal flaw.

Establishing universality in the group also allows group members and the leader to model acceptance. Similarities are the focus, not differences. One of the most important things the leader can do in establishing this factor is to help members recognize similarities. Not that the experiences necessarily have to be the same; it may be similarities of feelings about self or others or similarities in reactions or similarities in behaviors. The two most important components are focusing on similarities between members and modeling acceptance. Reducing feelings of isolation, strangeness, and shame promotes more open expressions of feelings and disclosing of important data.

Imparting of Information

Anyone who has worked with children in any capacity understands that they easily acquire misinformation and internalize experiences in unique ways. They use language in a personal way which can lead to misunderstandings. The value of this therapeutic factor cannot be underestimated when working with children, and a group setting provides a wonderful opportunity to deal with several aspects of imparting information at one time. There may even be similarities of misinformation or misperceptions for group members.

Another aspect of this factor is that it provides an opportunity to give new information. In addition to misunderstandings and misinformation, there may be ignorance. For example, in a personal growth group it may become evident that the members have little or no knowledge of the range of emotions leading to anger and rage. The group leader could point out that one first becomes irritated at something and begin to explore examples of irritation with members. The next step on the road to anger is annoyance, which could be defined as repeated irritations or irritations over time. And so on. While anger can be a reaction to a perceived threat to the integrity of the self, this is a deeper source of anger and unlikely to be dealt with adequately in brief counseling.

However, children can be taught how to deal with irritations and annoyances and keep them from becoming anger. *Why* one becomes irritated or annoyed may be beyond the scope of brief group therapy.

Altruism

Humans seem to thrive on being able to give to others. The idea that each of us has something worthwhile to others is a source of satisfaction. Often children are not made aware of what they can give to others that is of value and are generally put in the position of always receiving. Helping children become aware of what they can give to others that is of value is very rewarding as well as therapeutic. In brief group therapy, each member can give to as well as receive from others.

Yalom (1985) notes that the manifestation of altruism changes with the stage of the group. For example, in the beginning stages members are primarily concerned with safety issues and altruistic behavior may occur in the form of giving helpful suggestions and attending behaviors. In later stages it may take the form of supporting statements, and later still by "being with" others.

The group leader can certainly model these behaviors but can go further. Reinforcing these behaviors when they occur can help increase the frequency and quality. Focusing on the positive feelings that emerge when engaging in or receiving altruistic feedback will help group members recognize such behaviors and their intrinsic rewards. Finally, teaching children how to give and receive altruistic feedback may be a first step.

There is not much in the literature on the therapeutic factor of altruism. Erich Fromm (1956) proposed that

> to love one's flesh and blood is no achievement. The animal loves its young and cares for them. The helpless one loves his master, since his life depends on him; the child loves his parents, since he needs them. Only in the love of those who do not serve a purpose, love begins to unfold.

The Corrective Recapitulation of the Primary Family Group

In group counseling the group can function as a family and can also help members become aware of the impact of their family on their development. As the sessions go on, individuals become more consciously aware of the patterns for their family and the impact of these patterns on their current functioning.

Obviously, all of this takes considerable time to emerge and become useful in counseling. It is also clear that brief group counseling with children is unlikely to have enough sessions to make maximum use of this therapeutic factor. However, there are two aspects that may be useful, understanding relationships with parents and other relatives and what it is like to be in a family (the group) that is accepting and understanding.

Children, like adults, fall into patterns of relating and behaving without conscious thought. In particular, children tend to identify and act toward the new as they do to the known or old. For example, new adults in their world are not reacted toward as they objectively are, but are reacted to in terms of someone in the child's past (transference). The group setting can allow children to become better aware of the uniqueness of individuals and of the tendency to react to others in terms of their family relationships.

The atmosphere of the group is, in large part, the responsibility of the group leader. The leader is charged with being the person to model desired behaviors and to lead in setting norms and standards. Openness and acceptance as a worthwhile, unique individual may be a new experience for many children. They don't have to do anything special or have any particular characteristics in order to be accepted. The value of unconditional positive regard is sometimes underestimated in forming therapeutic relationships.

Brief group counseling's time constraints do not permit adequate unfolding of family patterns. The group leader needs to be very aware of how patterns in the group may be reflective of patterns in members' families and needs to foster a beginning awareness, for members, of how they react to new people in terms of old family relationships. The primary way this therapeutic factor can be used is by the leader having awareness of developing patterns, modeling and encouraging openness, acceptance and unconditional positive regard, and developing an understanding of the impact the family of origin has had on the development of the child.

Development of Socializing Techniques

The group setting can be an opportunity for members to learn social skills that will stand them in good stead in any situation. For some children, it may be the only time these skills are focused on and practiced. Further, socialization skills that are counterproductive can be brought to the individual's attention in a safe setting, in a caring way that helps acceptance of the feedback and ultimate use.

Many children do not have adequate opportunities to give and receive constructive feedback. Constructive feedback is that which is given to help the individual and not to satisfy some need or agenda of the giver of feedback. How to give constructive feedback will be discussed further in Chapter 4.

Happy, well-adjusted children are characterized by the degree to which they are accepted and liked by others and by a relatively high level of social-skills development. Thus, it is easy to see why development of socializing techniques can be a therapeutic factor in group counseling. Helping children to develop their social skills can also help them to be better liked and accepted by others.

Socialization skills in this context refer to being responsive to others in a way that promotes the relationship, having the ability to resolve conflicts in ways that are satisfying to all involved, able to sense and understand feelings of others, and having the ability to accept others in a nonjudgmental way. The group is an excellent way to bring these skills to the attention of members, practice the skills and to give and receive constructive feedback.

Imitative Behavior

The importance of the leader modeling desired behaviors has been discussed under the therapeutic factor of altruism. However, this is not the only source that members can learn from in the group; they can also learn from each other.

All members in any group are at different stages in their development, whether it is physical, cognitive, affective or social. Some will be further along than others. It is also possible that, for some things, children perceive the leader as being so far along in development that they could not hope to imitate the leader's behavior. In these cases, it would be more likely that a peer who is further along in his/her development would be perceived as the model. Both leaders and members can serve as models for desired behaviors.

Another effect of imitative behavior that is therapeutic is finding out that others may have had the same feelings, been in similar situations, or wondered about the same things. Not only have they been there, they have been able to work through, overcome, or resolve in ways that were beneficial. Knowing that others have done it gives encouragement that you can do it also.

Often this factor operates in indirect and ambiguous ways, that is, the leader does not consciously plan to have data emerge in the group that highlights how imitative behavior could be of benefit. It just happens. The leader needs to be aware that this factor may be helpful and make use of it in some way during the life of the group. Teaching children to look for and emulate positive models is something that can carry over into their development beyond the group.

Interpersonal Learning

The ability to develop interpersonal relationships appears to be tied into the quality of early relationships with caregivers, specifically the mother-child relationship. All of the object relation theorists focus on this relationship as crucial in the psychological development of the child.

Kohut (1971, 1977) proposed the importance of self-objects in the development of shame, guilt, envy, and so forth. Self-objects are those people in the child's life that become incorporated into the self of the child. These selfobjects provide the child with the sense of self, introject self-concept, and contribute to the development of the ability to relate to others. Kohut's work and others point out the significance of these early relationships in the development of borderline and narcissistic personality disorders.

Although brief group counseling is too short and not deep enough to undo deep-seated negative relationships, especially the mother-child one, it can provide support to the child to learn more positive ways of relating and the importance of developing positive relationships. It is sad, but these experiences may be some of the only positive ones for some children. It is very important for the group leader to plan interpersonal learning experiences that will help develop meaningful relationships.

Practicing relationship skills such as listening, responding, expressing feelings, and constructive confrontation can help children learn to relate in helpful ways. The ability to hear what the other person says and means makes them feel understood and valued. Responding in ways that communicate understanding fosters growth of relationships. These are skills that are simple, capable of being taught and learned, and have big payoffs in terms of developing positive relationships.

Not as easily learned are appropriate expressions of feelings. Some children are not allowed or encouraged to express feelings openly. Indeed, they may be chastised for expressing feelings and made to feel "wrong" for even having these feelings. The group may be the first and one of the only places where it is safe and expected for feelings to be expressed. Some techniques to encourage appropriate expression of feelings are in Chapters 8 and 9.

Yalom (1985) notes that "given enough time, every patient will begin to be him or herself. . . . There is no need for them to describe their pathology: they will sooner or later act it out." The key concept is time. Some individuals may be very adept at hiding their underlying problems/issues/concerns and it takes a long time before they act them out in the group. The time factor is certainly a constraint when doing brief counseling as there may not be enough time available to sit back and allow the problems/issues/concerns to emerge. The knowledgeable group leader can become adept at reading possible underlying problems/issues/concerns from interpersonal interactions in the group.

After some safety issues have been addressed adequately, interpersonal interactions in the group become reflective of relationships of members with others outside the group. Careful attention to patterns of relating, transferences, projections, and projective identifications can provide needed understandings of significant relationships outside the group and offer suggestions for fruitful interventions. The ability to observe and understand what is taking place in the group and the implications relies heavily on the education, experience, and empathy of the group leader. The clues are there but you have to be able to read them accurately.

Group Cohesiveness

A sense of belonging to a group reduces feelings of isolation. For children, being accepted as part of a group is an important part of the developmental process. Groups of all kinds play a significant role in children's lives and give them important feedback on how they are valued by others.

The same benefits accrue in brief group counseling. Children can experience what it is like to be accepted as they are, to be a part of a group that values each member, to not feel alone or apart from others, and to feel approved of and wanted. Members can become more open in expressing uncomfortable feelings with the knowledge that other members will not think them weird, tell them they are wrong to feel that way or in some way suggest that they shouldn't feel the way they do.

Growth in awareness of unexpressed feelings, the ability to trust others, and a more realistic concept of self can result from the group's cohesiveness. When there is cohesiveness members will demonstrate acceptance of others even when they disagree with them, participate freely, disclose relevant material, listen to others, give them support, and value the group experience.

Building group cohesiveness is a task begun by the group leader. Modeling trustworthiness, appropriate disclosure, blocking destructive behaviors, teaching listening and responding skills, providing an atmosphere conducive to expression of feelings all contribute to building group cohesion. Each of these tasks is discussed in more detail in Chapter 4.

Catharsis

Expression of feelings openly is very therapeutic, although mere expression may not be enough for growth to occur. Blocked feelings, repressed feelings, unacceptable feelings contribute to constricted development. Many children need to feel what it is like to be able to express positive or negative feelings and have the expression accepted as legitimate. That is, the feelings themselves are deemed to be the individual's own and, as such, are not subject to disapproval by others. The group may be the only place this happens for some children.

In addition to being able to express feelings openly, members may find that others have, or have had, similar feelings, thus producing feelings of similarity and connectedness to others. Learning to appropriately express positive and negative feelings is part of the interpersonal process and contributes to developed meaningful relationships. Trust is built when members can rely on the honest expression of feelings.

The group leader must become aware of the impact of feeling expression on group members. It may be beneficial for someone to express angry feelings, for example, but other members of the group may feel threatened by angry feelings. Noting reactions to expression of feelings by all members in the group provides clues to the degree of acceptance of these feelings, possible personal issues/concerns, and if there are others with similar feelings.

Group leaders must be able to deal with personal anxieties raised by the expression of some feelings. They must be comfortable with their own feeling expression, able to handle intense affect and, above all, not block the open expression of feelings.

Existential Factors

Children are not immune to existential factors. Although they may not be able to articulate them adequately, they experience these factors and there are indirect ways to detect them. (For suggestions, see the chapter on fairy tales.)

The existential concerns of life being unfair and unjust at times, pain as a part of life, death as inevitable, assuming responsibility and accepting aloneness as a human condition all appear in children as well as in adults. The group leader can best use these factors by becoming acutely aware that they do exist for children and are expressed in a variety of ways, by tuning in to expressions of concern that have existential implications, and by helping children to understand and accept that these conditions affect everyone and can never be wholly resolved. Group sessions can provide support for children who are only dimly aware of having these concerns, teach them existential issues that are universal, and help them learn to deal with them in a constructive way.

Being the leader of a group that has only a few sessions for a life span is very demanding. If the group is to be effective for the members, use of these therapeutic factors is crucial. It calls for a high level of awareness and expertise on the part of the leader and demands a continuing examination of self to gain more knowledge that contributes to self-growth as well as to effective group counseling.

4

The Group Leader and Group Dynamics

While there are many factors that contribute to successful outcomes for groups, none is more important than the group leader. In addition to education, training and experience, personal characteristics, attitudes, and awarenesses are important. Group facilitation skills grow from these noncognitive characteristics.

For purposes of discussion, factors for the leader will be divided into two categories; those that can be directly taught, termed *skills*; and those that are inherent in the individual and can only be enhanced and expanded, termed *characteristics*. Major skills are defined as attending, listening and responding, observational, emotional expressiveness, confrontation, blocking, linking, interpreting, probing, clarifying, summarizing, and giving constructive feedback. Characteristics are defined as warmth, caring, acceptance of self and others, genuineness, risk-taking, hopefulness, and belief in the process. An interaction of skills and characteristics is basic to using group process effectively.

SKILLS

Active Listening and Responding

Effective development of group facilitation skills rests on the degree to which active listening and responding abilities are fostered. These skills promote perceptions of empathy and feeling understood promotes development of trust in the group. Carkuff and Berenson (1977) have produced considerable evidence that these skills are crucial, no matter which theoretical orientation is practiced. Active listening is defined as hearing and understanding the content and the underlying feelings accompanying the message. Responding is the critical part of active listening, for it is the mechanism, or means, whereby the therapist conveys his/her understanding.

Attending

Attending is a behavior that helps convey active listening and understanding. It is defined as paying attention to the other in such a way that the other feels he/she has the counselor's total attention. Being fully there in the relationship is another way to define attending. Observable physical behaviors convey attending, and behaviors such as eye contact, body turned to the person, a slight forward lean are examples of physical attending.

Observational Skills

Observational skills take some time to develop in the group leader as there are several members in the group and it is certainly more difficult to observe several individuals adequately, but the ability to do so enhances tuning in to group process. The key parts of observational skills are becoming aware of and understanding nonverbal communication, as it is the major part of the message or messages. Nonverbal behaviors provide clues for the individual in the group as well as for the group as a whole.

Observing verbal shifts in dialogue can also be important to understanding what is happening in the group. Noting who talks to whom, who suddenly stops or starts talking, and especially deflections are useful skills for the group leader. Resistances, subgrouping, development of cliques can be used advantageously if the group leader has high observational skills which will allow positive interventions before these behaviors become problems.

Emotional Expressiveness

Emotional expressiveness is an important skill for the leader to model for group members. Children need to develop skills in appropriate expression of feelings. The group leader needs to have a heightened awareness of his/her personal feelings and the ability and willingness to express them appropriately. For example, seeing an adult express intense emotions in a way that is not destructive to others teaches the child not only that it can be done, but also, how to do it. For many children, this group experience may be one of the few opportunities they have to observe an adult with emotional expressiveness they can imitate profitably.

Achieving basic skills of attending, active listening and responding, observation, and emotional expressiveness allows the next group of skills to be developed. The next group are confrontational skills, giving constructive feedback, blocking, linking, interpreting, probing, clarifying, and summarizing. Brief definitions follow.

Confrontation

Confrontation is defined as an *invitation* to the other person to examine his/her behavior and its impact on you or on others. It is not an attack, should not be done when there is intense emotion, and should be suggested *only* to help the other person become more effective. The group leader can use confrontation most effectively after the therapeutic relationship has been developed and trust has been fostered in the group. Confrontation is a skill that relies on the awareness of the confronter of when, where, and how to confront so that the person being confronted can make good use of the information.

Constructive Feedback

Constructive feedback is most helpful if the receiver of the feedback can understand what is being communicated. That sounds somewhat elementary, but all too often feedback is too indirect or vague to be of much use. Constructive feedback is most helpful if it is nonjudgmental, is focused on observable behavior, and when the giver of feedback makes sure the receiver heard what was said and meant.

Blocking

Blocking, used appropriately, is a skill that contributes to the progress of the group. Blocking storytelling, attacks, and inappropriate communications or behaviors are examples of positive uses of the skill. Inappropriate use is usually related to countertransference issues of the group leader. For example, the leader may be very uncomfortable with open expressions of anger and thus, blocks any expression of anger by group members. The leader has to be very aware of his/her possible countertransference issues and their impact on the functioning of the group.

Linking

Linking is a process whereby similarities among group members are brought into the group's awareness, themes of sessions identified, and group process understood. The ability to use linking is a highly developed skill that needs time and training. Awarenesses by the group leader together with understanding and interpretation promote development of linking skills. This is how the group leader understands process, that is, what is taking place in the group between members. The greatest part of understanding relies on process and not on content.

Interpreting

Interpreting is defined for this book as the leader telling the group what he/she observes and understands that the group is doing, for example, avoiding expressing intense negative emotions. It may involve making group members aware of what each of them is contributing to the group's progress or lack of progress, how the group as a whole is functioning, how the group makes decisions, how it may be colluding, or how it is addressing a common issue. For example, the content of verbalizations in the group may be about school and the leader interprets for the group that they are really discussing safety issues for the group. This use of interpretation is an important part of making the process unfolding in the group known and understood by group members.

Probing

Probing or questioning should be used sparingly if at all. The group leader is more effective if he/she makes statements instead of questioning. Indeed, many questions are rhetorical, designed to lead the person being questioned to a foregone conclusion. Group leaders should limit probing to those times when more information is essential to understanding what the group member is experiencing *at that time*, and not in order to know more about the situation or people involved. Probing can quickly allow the group experience to become a there-and-then one instead of having a here-and-now focus.

Clarifying

Clarifying is intended to help group members understand each other better or to clear up misperceptions or misunderstandings. Checking to ensure clear communication facilitates the development of trust and understanding. Teaching children not to make assumptions, but to make sure what was heard was what was meant, is an important accomplishment. Relationships are strengthened by clear, direct, and accurate communications.

Summarizing

Summarizing during and at the end of sessions helps group members better understand what they are doing and accomplishing. It is similar in some ways to linking skills because it pulls together aspects of what the group did into an understandable concept. Summarizing can link what has taken place in previous sessions, which makes group members more aware of what the group's issues really are. Content is seldom an accurate or direct portrayal of underlying issues or concerns. Through summarizing the group leader interprets for members. Another task summarizing accomplishes when used at the beginning of a session is to help group members recapture some of the affect of the previous session. Therapeutic work can begin quicker when unresolved affect is accessed.

CHARACTERISTICS

Some leader characteristics that contribute to forming therapeutic relationships and fostering group cohesiveness are not easily taught, if they can be taught at all. Characteristics such as warmth, caring, acceptance of self and others, genuineness, risk-taking, hopefulness, and belief in the process are internal states and attitudes. External events and experiences play a part in forming these characteristics but the individual is in control and can only be encouraged by others to develop these characteristics. However, better communication of some of these characteristics can be taught.

Genuineness

Genuineness in the therapist is crucial because, if trust is to develop, group members must believe the leader is free from deceit or hypocrisy. It is possible to mask real feelings or act differently from that which is felt; however, the sham is difficult to sustain and may not fool anyone for very long. Countertransference issues play a role in the ability to be genuine. Group members have to be able to trust the leader to be authentic if they are expected to trust in the process to help with the problem or concern.

Hopefulness

A group leader who is not hopeful and convinced that people can and do get better will not be able to instill hopefulness in group members. Instillation of hope is a group therapeutic factor (Yalom, 1985) and helps to encourage group members. An attitude that acknowledges the intensity or severity of the problem/concern, and also conveys a sense of hopefulness can be inspiring. The attitude must be genuine and consistent with reality. Giving false hope or not recognizing limitations or constraints is counterproductive.

Risk-taking

The group leader must be prepared to take psychological risks. That means allowing for mistakes and acting on hunches. One must be willing to enter unknown and uncharted territory not fully understanding what to expect—to paraphrase the "Star Trek" opening line, "to boldly go where you have not gone before." Always playing it safe and only doing that which has been done before will not model appropriate risk-taking behavior for group members, nor will it enhance progress for the group.

Faith in Group Process

Faith in group process develops over time with proper education and experiences. Belief that the process does work allows the leader a great deal of latitude and gives some of the responsibility for the group to the members. The leader is not solely responsible for the group and group members are empowered instead of being in a subordinate position. While the leader has certain responsibility for group progress, the interaction between members is mainly the responsibility of members. The leader facilitates but does not dictate process.

Warmth and Caring

Warmth and caring can be communicated through nonverbal behaviors such as tone of voice, facial expression, and nonverbal behaviors that make the other person feel cared for. Group leaders must take care that their faces say "I'm glad to see you" or "Welcome." A blank look or frown doesn't convey warmth.

The group leader's facial expressions should mirror his/her internal states when appropriate. It is helpful if the expression on the face is congruent with what is being experienced as empathy. Under these circumstances, no one has to say "I understand"; the face says it all and is a more accurate reflection of empathy than are the words.

Caring for the other has as its basis nonjudgmental positive regard. That is, while you may not approve of or accept the other's behavior(s), he/she is still accepted and appreciated as a unique, worthwhile individual. Group members can sense when they are cared for and feeling cared for promotes trust.

Some leader nonverbal behaviors that convey caring are insuring privacy for group meetings, setting the room up for the session prior to its start, and adhering to time boundaries, that is, beginning and ending on time.

Acceptance of Self and Others

Acceptance of self leads to greater acceptance of others and their uniqueness. Understanding who you are and how you came to be that way allows for better acceptance of all parts of self, even the parts you don't particularly like. Liking and acceptance are not the same thing. You can accept something you don't like. Greater acceptance of self reduces countertransferences because of deeper understanding of personal issues and transferences.

Group members need to feel accepted for themselves as they are. Change is usually the result of a decision by the individual and lasting change seldom results from external pressure. Therefore, if the group leader expects positive changes to take place for group members, it is essential that the group member(s) commit to change(s). Group members are more likely to commit to change after trust and the therapeutic relationship have developed and these begin with group members able to see that they are accepted as they are and given the freedom to choose.

GUIDELINES FOR THE GROUP LEADER

Although the most important element for effective group leadership is the personhood or selfhood of the leader, there are also important leader attitudes and behaviors that enhance group process. The following discussion of behaviors is not intended to be an exhaustive one; it focuses on certain behaviors that reflect attitudes, promotes self-reflection for group members, facilitates communication between members, and helps use the resources in and of the group to work with individuals. Not all skills or behaviors need be present in every session. Many are, but some should be used after a therapeutic relationship has been developed. If used before members have developed trust in the leader, the group, and the process, there is a tendency to resist and retreat. Timing is important.

Group Focus

Goal(s) and purpose(s) of session made clear to members. The leader has a responsibility to focus each session on accomplishing a part of the overall goal for the group. Each session has a goal that is consistent with the overall goal. While it is not necessary to always begin with stating the goal for the session, at some point members should understand the purpose.

It is essential for the leader to have clear goals and purposes. Proper preplanning can take care of most goal-setting; however, groups don't always run according to plan and adjustments have to be made.

Focusing the group. Sessions don't need to be rigidly structured, but they do need to be kept focused so that goals can be accomplished. When members start to stray, a gentle reminder of what the focus is may be enough. If, however, the group continues to stray, resistance is probably a consideration. The task of the leader then is to point out that there is resistance and to try to identify what triggered it.

Another component of focus is staying present-centered. When members begin to focus on there and then, the group leader should refocus on the here and now. This here-and-now focus does not mean the past cannot be used; it does mean that the past should be brought into the present and reexperienced. Techniques to encourage a here-and-now focus include using present tense, expressing feelings about the event as if they are occurring now, and making "I" statements.

Using the present tense forces attention on here-and-now experiencing. For example, saying "I had an upsetting experience yesterday" keeps it in the there and then. Saying "I am upset" brings it into the present and forces an awareness of the intensity of affect connected to the experience. Whenever events are "talked about" the intensity of feelings experienced is dampened. Lessening this intensity allows for easier ignoring, suppression, repression or denial. These defenses do not permit closure but promote development of unfinished business.

Encouraging reexperiencing of feelings surrounding the event allows for clarification, understanding and, perhaps, some resolution. The real intensity of the affect can be safely dealt with in the group and the potential for damage to the individual and relationships controlled. Members are also taught that intense feelings need not be destructive but can be expressed in such a way that leads to resolution and strengthening of relationships.

Making "I" statements forces an awareness of personal responsibility for feelings. That is, so-and-so did not make you angry (this is past tense), you are angry. The combination of "I" statements and present tense is conducive to staying present-centered. It also blocks storytelling by keeping the focus on the individual and his/her experiencing rather than concentrating on other elements in the situation.

Providing adequate structure. Specific guidelines for how much structure to provide are difficult to formulate. Too much structure interferes with development of relationships in the group. Too little structure and members flounder. Some leaders provide so much structure that members leave without having done real therapeutic work on their issues/concerns. They may have been active and enjoyed the sessions but little of a therapeutic nature was accomplished. This format tends to meet the needs of the leader to have activity and a pleasant experience that everyone enjoys.

Exercises are too often misused in this way. They are not used as a mechanism to deepen awareness and understanding but to make a point or to make sure time is filled. A certain amount of tension or discomfort encourages interaction. Too much comfort and nothing much occurs that is therapeutic or growth.

Expressions of feeling. Group leaders encourage appropriate expressions of feelings, understanding that this expression is cathartic. Appropriateness is related to stage of group development, ability of group members to tolerate expression of intense affect, level of self-awareness, and defense mechanisms in operation.

Group also provides an opportunity to teach members how to become more aware of feelings that are less intense, such as irritation, not just intense ones like anger. Learning milder feelings can also lead to dealing with them before they build up in intensity and become overwhelming or out of control.

The group may be the only place that some members can express feelings openly without fear of being told they are "wrong" or "bad." The leader helps to develop an environment where feeling expression is safe and encouraged. Feelings are discussed in more detail in Chapters 8 and 9.

Identifies and clarifies themes, goals, struggles and/or conflicts for members. Most group members will not have clear goals and one leader task is to help clarify personal goals of members. These are not what the leader perceives to be their goals, but what emerges for each member. Even children who recognize that they have problems just want the pain to stop and everything to become "right" or "good." They are very similar to adults in this regard.

Groups tend to develop themes even when it appears that members are working on very different problems/concerns. These themes may be related to individual issues, or to the group-as-a-whole. Understanding the theme helps the leader to better guide the group.

Themes for group members are identified by linking together what individuals have said (within individual theme). They may have identified their real issue (as opposed to the presenting one) over time by what they have verbalized in the group. They may not be fully aware of the underlying issue but the theme for the individual usually identifies it.

Group-as-a-whole themes are identified by becoming aware of what the group is doing or avoiding. Are members talking about the same basic issue/problem/concern from varying perspectives? For example, one member may talk about playground behavior, another about what happens in the classroom, another about their neighborhood, and someone else about home. Listening carefully to what feelings are being expressed about these situations may lead to identifying something such as safety needs as the theme. Content is much less important than feelings when trying to identify group themes.

Promote interaction between members. There is a tendency for communication to be funneled through the leader. Children are used to the adult being the authority figure and will, most likely, need to be taught and encouraged to speak directly to each other. This is a valuable skill for members to learn, how to communicate with each other. Communication involves sharing of opinions, thought, or feelings and knowing how to receive the opinions, thoughts, and feelings of others. Undesirable communication patterns such as interrupting others, name-calling, labeling, lashing out, judging, and so on may have to be unlearned.

Group leaders can encourage interaction between members by asking them to tell each other what they are feeling or thinking. Instead of having these expressions to the leader or to the group, ask that they select one member to receive their expression of feeling or thought. Another possibility is to encourage members to give feedback to each other. When a member expresses a feeling or thought, other members can be encouraged to respond directly about their reaction(s) to what was expressed. This is one way support is given by group members and the focus is not primarily on the leader.

Group Leaders' Reports

A good habit to develop is to write a short report about each session. Writing a report that addresses basic group dynamics helps the leader to identify themes, resistances, and defense mechanisms. Suggested group dynamics are level of participation, feeling tone of the group, communication patterns, nonverbal behavior, and resistances.

Level of participation points out who actively participated and who had low levels of participation. If there are shifts in how much a member participates, the leader can seek to understand when the shift occurred. Did it happen during the session or was there an outside-the-group reason? If the shift was not observed during the session, the leader may wish to bring it up in the next session. Bringing it up in the group gives members an opportunity to focus on and express what they are experiencing.

Groups may experience several feeling tones throughout a session. By reflecting on the dominant or persistent feeling tone, the leader tunes in to the process, that is, what is happening between group members. This is not always expressed directly or even known consciously by members. The leader can bring the process to awareness for members once it is identified, and looking at the feeling tone of the group for that session helps to do so.

Communication patterns can reveal members who are included or excluded. Note which members are talked to and which are ignored. When a member makes a comment or observation is it responded to or ignored? Is there a tendency for two or three members to be supportive of each other? This may be a clique developing. Are there members who talk only to or through the leader? In order for group cohesion to develop, members have to feel included in the group. The leader needs to intervene if members are being excluded, and noting communication patterns is one way of becoming aware of inclusion or exclusion.

Nonverbal behaviors are more revealing of what the individual is experiencing than verbalizations. Facial expression, body movement or nonmovement, body positions, shifts, and dissonance are clues to this inner experiencing.

Facial expressions can be very revealing. Many children have not yet learned to mask their feelings and their faces are very revealing of inner states. Carefully looking at expressions and learning to read them help the leader to understand when members are experiencing intense or frightening affect that members may find difficult or unable to verbalize. Helping them to express and deal with this affect is therapeutic.

Sudden changes in body positions can be indicators of inner conflict or turmoil. Stillness when previously there was much movement, or lots of shifting around in the chair after sitting quietly may indicate that a sensitive area has been touched on or neared.

Significant differences between verbalizations and nonverbal behaviors may indicate intense affect that is being suppressed. For example, saying you are angry but smiling is dissonance. Smiling is an attempt to nullify or deny the intensity of the anger. The leader can point out how confusing communications are when there is this kind of dissonance.

Some resistances may be difficult to detect when the group is in session. Focusing on identifying resistances when writing session notes may help the leader to become more aware of them and, more important, what triggered them. Resistances do not have to be addressed directly all of the time. Sometimes the resistance is exhibited in defense of the ego and in fulfilling that function is basic to the existence of the individual at that time. These should be noted by the leader for his/her understanding but not addressed to the individual either directly or indirectly. Much more information is needed before bringing it to the attention of the individual.

Some resistances are shared by group members and may indicate shared problems/concerns/issues that underlie the presenting problem. It may be useful to use this data to point out similarities. At other times, shared resistances indicate when the group is resisting something. Reflection on this by the leader can clarify what is happening in the group to produce resistance and help suggest how to intervene.

Group Process and Commentary

Understanding and using group process facilitate group cohesion and productiveness. Process refers to what is happening between members and within the group at the present time (Yalom, 1985). Learning to make process commentary is developed over time and demands a high level of skill. Leaders that are proficient in process commentary are able to help the group be more productive and, thereby, benefit individual group members.

How does the leader identify process? Some interpretation of just what the group is doing is made by the leader based on observations and leader's feelings. Observing levels of participation and any shifts in participation by members, communication patterns, nonverbal communication, feeling tone in the group, noting what is talked about and what is avoided, and feelings expressed or blocked give clues to group process.

Observations noted above facilitate the leader's ability to identify specific areas of struggle and conflict in the group, confront members when topics are switched or they refuse to acknowledge intense affect, and identify and clarify what members are saying or asking for in indirect, disguised ways. Commentary should focus on what the group is doing or avoiding, not on individual members, and should be brief and present-centered. The immediacy of commentary is essential and more useful to members. "Talking about" what occurred previously tends to lessen intensity and members are better able to maintain their resistances and defenses.

Techniques for Process Commentary

Attention must also be given to the manner in which the commentary is given. After all, the goal is to get the group moving without making members defensive and withdrawn. Important considerations are the stage of group development and maturity level of members.

It is not constructive or productive to make process commentary before group members have established a therapeutic relationship with each other and the leader. The only exception would be if members had participated in groups before and were familiar with process commentary. There is a tendency for members to take the comments personally and to feel that they are doing something "wrong" or "bad." Instead of exploring and understanding their behavior, they immediately try to change it to that which they perceive the leader to want.

Maturity level of members refers primarily to the level of development as a group member. Most often, maturity is a result of experience as a group member. There may be a few people who have this maturity level when they first participate in a group, but not many.

The leader can promote acceptance of process commentary by framing comments in a supportive way (i.e., by not labeling the behavior, by appreciating and neutralizing defenses, by making "I" statements, and by being tentative.) As in constructive confrontation, the emotional state of group members should be taken into consideration when framing a process commentary. Intense affect distorts communication and the commentary could be easily misunderstood. If the intent is to diffuse or dampen the intensity of feelings, dialogue should continue until it is clear that the message received is the one that was intended.

Frame the commentary in such a way that it does not label or evaluate the behavior. Choose words that describe what you have observed and a possible interpretation, but take care not to give the impression that you disapprove of what you have observed. Members are more apt to be willing to consider your interpretation if they don't feel that you are disappointed in them.

Remember that members will very likely become defensive after a process commentary as you are asking them to confront a resistance or an anxiety. Confronting either of these is threatening and uncomfortable, hence, members try to avoid doing so. Knowing that defensiveness is likely, you can decide what to focus on and how to phrase it in such a way that members can be more accepting of the commentary.

When making a process commentary, make it personal by making "I" statements. Do not say anything that conveys blame or criticism. If you use "I" statements, you are allowing members some leeway to accept or reject the commentary and giving them permission to do so. By doing so, they will be more open to accepting your commentary because it is not imposed. Even if you are correct in your analysis, if members don't accept and act on it nothing useful occurs and there may even be some loss of group.

Being correct is useful only when members make constructive use of the information.

Be somewhat tentative in making the process commentary and put it forth as a possible hypothesis. You will be correct under most circumstances but there is the possibility that you are not correct in your analysis. Tentativeness allows for discussion, clarification and, when they are ready, acceptance. Further, if members are not able to accept it at that point, they are more likely to continue to consider the possibility that you are correct and act on it at a later time.

Three examples are presented. A group situation that most leaders encounter, a process commentary, and an analysis. An example of a nongroup process commentary will also be presented.

Group Situation

The third session for a group of 5th-grade children begins and it is difficult to get the group focused on group concerns. They are chatting about an upcoming class event and resist all efforts to focus the group in the here and now.

Process commentary. "The group seems to be more comfortable talking about outside events. What isn't safe about being here and interacting in a more present-centered way?"

A more direct commentary would be "It's safer for members to be outside the group today."

Analysis. Members usually resist being present-centered because, for example, they don't feel safe to disclose, are avoiding intense affect, or are engaging in a power struggle with the leader. There may be other reasons, but these are some major ones. There may also be individual reasons; however, if the whole group or the majority is resisting here-and-now interaction, focus for commentary should be on what the group is doing.

Nonprocess commentary. "What are you avoiding or resisting?" "The group doesn't want to work today." "This class event is more important to you than the group."

All of these responses may be accurate observations. However, they, in some way, blame group members and this will likely make them defensive. The group has only had two sessions and members may not be ready or able to respond to a direct question on resistance, particularly if they have little or no experience as group members.

Situation 2

The fourth meeting for eight-year-olds lapses into silence after a lively exchange of feelings on an issue. No one says anything and it looks like the silence will continue.

Process commentary. "The intenseness of the interaction has stirred up some anxious feelings. Are you wondering if I can take care of you?"

Analysis. Whenever intense affect is stirred up, individuals may be concerned about their ability to control their affect and may experience anxiety. The anxiety could be about being overwhelmed by intense feelings, unable to control them, feeling safe about expressing them, or wondering if the person in authority will take care of them. The individual anxiety is probably shared by all or most group members because the entire group is responding by being silent, not just one or two members. All of a sudden, it doesn't feel safe enough for members.

Nonprocess commentary. "I guess you're comfortable with the silence." "Why did the group fall silent? Are you resisting something?"

Neither of these responses interprets the behavior of the group in order to remove the block. While they may indeed be resisting, asking if they are resisting is unlikely to receive a yes response. It is more likely to result in members feeling that they have done something wrong.

Situation 3

The group had a very productive second session where many positive feelings were exchanged and interactions took place. It is now the middle of the third session and the leader wonders what happened to all the positive feelings generated in the last session.

For the past 20 minutes the group could be termed "cranky." There is much interrupting of others, changing the topic, discounting of each other, and so on.

Process commentary. "The group is making sure that they don't get closer to each other or become intimate. It's difficult to get close to someone who is cranky and its easy to keep others at a distance by being cranky."

Analysis. People often want to step back from becoming intimate. Unsure about their acceptance of and by others, fear of someone getting too close, being threatened by intimacy are some reasons for withdrawing. This is taking place on an unconscious level so that they are unaware of the significance of what they are doing, cannot say it directly, and so use an indirect method to accomplish their goal. The group-as-a-whole in Situation 3 is collectively retreating and withdrawing.

Nonprocess commentary. "Boy, this group is cranky today!" "Why are group members interrupting each other, calling names, etc.? Last week you seemed to like each other." "Our group rules specify that we will not interrupt each other or call names. Why are you breaking group rules?"

These commentaries do not interpret the group's behavior for them. Members are put in a position of defending their behavior rather than exploring the consequences of it in the group. There is also an element of blame attached to the responses, and blaming usually results in withdrawal or defense. Neither of these behaviors furthers group progress.

Group process commentary is intended to remove an obstacle to group progress. The group is stuck in some way, or unaware of implications or impact of some collective behavior(s) on progress. Process commentary is direct, succinct, interpretative in the sense of suggesting a possible reason for the group's behavior.

5

Creating a Group

There are several important points to consider before creating and facilitating a group. First and foremost is the purpose of the group. That is, why create and conduct a group? What will the group do for individual members? What therapeutic goals are expected to be accomplished via the group?

PURPOSE OF GROUPS

The two primary reasons for therapeutic groups for children are response to needs and prevention. Response to needs includes support groups, theme-focused groups, such as children of alcoholics, and behavioral change, such as fighting. Prevention includes personal growth groups, educational groups, communication skill development and guidance groups, and career exploration. There may be some overlapping of these categories; however, one or the other should be the primary purpose or goal for the group.

All else flows from establishing a clear purpose for the group. Selection of members, strategies, and techniques are tasks that are facilitated through a clear understanding of the purpose of the group. Group members are selected on the basis of their fit with the purpose, that is, does the child have a need for this type of group. Strategies and techniques will be selected as those which will enhance the purpose and the leader's self-preparation should be consistent with the purpose of the group.

For example, if a group was being created to provide support for children who were physically abused then children who were not physically abused would not be selected to participate. Strategies would be developed to enable them to understand that they did nothing to cause the abuse, and techniques used would help to integrate the cognitive and affective understanding of their situations.

A therapeutic group is a creation. It does not come into being until someone, usually the group's leader, takes steps to cause it to exist, and each group is unique. No two groups are exactly alike, even if membership and the leader do not change. Members change cognitively and affectively. Goals and purposes change. Viewing each group as a new creation helps to understand how important each step is so that each group created will maximize its potential.

Bringing a group into existence involves a great deal of knowledge and understanding on the part of the leader. Putting all the elements together that compose an effective and efficient group is not easily done; it involves a lot of thought, time, and effort. The primary tasks are taking care of environmental concerns, planning sessions, screening potential group members, and pre-preparation for group.

ENVIRONMENTAL CONCERNS

Environmental concerns refer to securing a place for meetings and setting the time and duration for sessions. Where group sessions are held can dictate the degree of comfort members will feel, not only physically, but also psychologically. The room should ensure privacy above all other concerns. Members need to feel that they will not be observed or overheard. Lack of intrusive noises also contributes to a feeling of a safe environment. Seating should be as comfortable as possible without desks as barriers. Group leaders may wish to keep eight to ten folding chairs available for those spaces where it is not possible to have seats without desks.

Decisions have to be made on how many sessions to hold and the time needed for each session. These decisions will be constrained by the setting and age of participants. Only under exceptional circumstances should sessions be moved. That is, all sessions for a particular group should be held in the same place. Therefore, the leader should confirm the availability of the space for all sessions before the group begins. The younger and more immature the group members are, the shorter each session should be. Recommended time limits are 30 minutes for younger children, to 50 minutes for children who can handle the longer time span.

SCREENING GROUP MEMBERS

Children are usually referred for counseling by teachers because of concerns about their behavior. Behaviors such as aggression toward others, withdrawal, inability to stay seated or focused on the lesson, reactions to life situations or crises, depression, stealing, lying, and inability to get along with peers are examples. While others may also refer children, the referral usually comes from someone who has had an opportunity to observe the behavior.

Before considering the child for group, the leader should observe the child in the classroom or on the playground and consult with the teacher at a minimum. It is useful to consult with parents also, for several reasons. It involves parents in the process, can aid in securing their cooperation and permission, and can verify behavior(s).

There are also standardized behavioral rating instruments. Most are used by adults, such as teachers and parents, to rate the child on observed behaviors. Clusters of behaviors emerge and are compared with normative groups. The fit between ratings for a particular child and various norm groups can present a profile that can be identified with suggested interventions. Further, the frequency of behaviors and agreement between raters also provide relevant information. One instrument, the Jessness (1962), has the child rate him/herself in addition to the teacher and/or parents. This makes it possible to determine the extent of agreement or disagreement between how the child sees him/herself and how he/she is perceived by others. A behavioral rating instrument could also be used as part of the decision-making process.

Another fruitful source of information is school records. Aptitude, ability, attendance patterns, number of schools attended, and so on are all provided in cumulative records. Comments by previous teachers, disciplinary problems/actions may also be in the records. All of this information helps round out a picture of the child.

Interviewing

The next step in screening is an individual interview with each potential group member. The purpose of the interview is to assess readiness for participation in group. Ego strength, adequate verbalization skills, cooperativeness, and the ability to pay attention and be focused can be evaluated through the interview.

The group leader should also be the interviewer, although there should be no mention of a possible membership in a group. The interview should focus on getting acquainted. Drawing materials or play dough can be provided for the child to work with while talking. This activity relaxes most children and they begin to talk more freely and openly.

Begin with asking about school-related issues. What they like, dislike, find easy to do or hard to do are fairly nonthreatening enough to allow most children to willingly answer. You will also be interested in knowing how they perceive their relationships with peers. From this, you can move on to perceptions and feelings about relationships with authority figures, such as teachers. There is little or no emphasis on the family at this point unless the child initiates the discussion.

After gathering information and conducting the interview, a decision can be made on appropriateness for group. If the answer is no, consider what alternative might be better, such as individual sessions. Some conditions that may not be readily handled or addressed in group are too short an attention span, excessive dependence, active displays of hostility, disabling conditions that would put them at a disadvantage in group, being under treatment by other mental health professionals where this group would interfere with treatment, or chronic illness that may prevent them from attending sessions.

After choosing children to be in the group, write a letter to parents requesting their permission for participation. Any other specific procedures mandated by the agency or school should also be followed.

PREVENTING PROBLEM BEHAVIORS

Common problems that are encountered in groups with children fall loosely into two categories: inappropriate or ineffective communications, and physical distractions. Included in communications are such behaviors as interrupting other members, making disparaging comments, name-calling, silence, monopolizing, and calling someone or something stupid or other inappropriate remarks.

Physical distractions that interrupt group process include hitting others, inability to stay seated, nervous mannerisms that are distracting, and nonverbal behaviors that suggest that they have withdrawn from the group.

Some behaviors in each category can be addressed and/or prevented by adequately preparing group members prior to conducting the group. Pre-preparation not only involves planning the sessions and interviewing or screening members, it can also be teaching group membership skills. Children do not usually come into group knowing how to be a member unless they have had experience or have been taught to do so. Being a member of a group is different than being a member of a social group or of a class. Too often, little time or thought is given to preparing members for group.

While preparation will not prevent disruptive or unproductive behavior from always happening, it can help limit the frequency and intensity of these behaviors. Many can be anticipated if attention is given to individuals who will be in the group as their characteristic behavior outside the group is reflective of how you can expect them to relate and act within the group. Suggestions for pre-preparation follow.

TOPICS FOR PRE-PREPARATION FOR GROUP

When preparing children to participate in group, plan to hold an individual session and, if possible, a group session. The individual session will cover topics such as individual goals, group goals, how the group will work, expectations of group members, and it will answer questions children may have.

Setting individual goals helps the child see how his/her needs will fit in and be taken care of, which helps promote trust and safety. Further, having specific goals to work toward provides needed structure so that feelings of floundering may be alleviated. Ask what would they like to get out of the sessions, what do they want to work on that is personal to them, and how will they know what they have accomplished. Try to help them set goals that are realistic, obtainable, and measurable or observable in some way. Having a goal to increase self-esteem is admirable, but what will be observable or measurable to let them know that the goal has been reached? Setting individual goals produces another benefit, that of giving the child some decision-making power and control. This is one of the first steps in helping children to learn to assume responsibility.

Give some brief explanation of how the group is expected to work. Cover topics such as theme or focus of the group, what can be talked about in the group, and some expected outcomes. Since each group will be different and membership changes, it is difficult to predict just what will happen in the group, but some things can be anticipated and explained. These explanations will help reduce anxiety and fears.

Describe some of the expectations of group members, focusing on those behaviors that will help them get the most out of their group experience. Some basic expectations are: to participate in group sessions; allow others to express their feelings without judging them right or wrong, bad or good; decide for yourself how much to disclose and when to disclose; pay attention to your feelings and express them in words; experiment with new behaviors in the group; and maintain confidentiality. Other topics that may be discussed are not interrupting others, storytelling, name-calling, making disparaging comments, or hitting others. This is also a good time to explore with individual children what they feel could be done to help them feel safe in the group.

Confidentiality is somewhat difficult to ensure, as the leader will have little or no control over what members say or discuss outside the group. Given this constraint, it is important to stress confidentiality, teach the members what can and cannot be discussed outside the group, and make sure they know that confidentiality cannot be mandated, it can only be encouraged. Confidentiality is easier to maintain if members know how to discuss process outside the group without telling any personal information.

How to help members understand the difference between process and content develops over time. It is essential that group leaders understand the distinction, for if they do not, they cannot communicate the difference to group members. A simplified explanation is that process is what happens with and between members in the group, and content is what they talk about. For example, when the group goes through a get-acquainted exercise, sets group goals, and talks about safety issues, these are all process and can be discussed outside the group. However, if members talk about what happened to them that makes them sad or not feel safe, this is content and should not be discussed outside the group.

Group leaders should be aware that parents, teachers, and group members' friends all will want to know something about what is going on in the group. If the child is not able to say anything, the worst may be assumed, and others will feel that it may be discussed, usually unfavorably. Suspicion and probing of group members are not conducive to productive groups. If the child does reveal content, and it becomes known to the group, then trust is destroyed. Most persons outside the group will be satisfied knowing the process and procedures.

This is also an appropriate time to develop a contract with the child, a contract delineating what is expected of the leader and of the child as a group member. The contract should be short, simple, and cover most topics covered in the interview, such as attendance. Both sign the contract.

PLANNING FOR GROUP

Develop a plan for the group based on needs of group members as determined from consultation with teachers and/or parents, school records, behavior rating scales, and the interview. The plan should specify goals, tentative objectives and strategies, rules and guidelines, and the plan for evaluation.

Prior to developing a plan, the group leader should consult professional literature to either refresh knowledge or gain knowledge relevant to needs of group members. New findings are being developed constantly that help understandings and suggest new strategies that are useful. The leader has the responsibility to be as knowledgeable as possible about human growth and development, the specific needs of group members and how these needs developed, tested techniques or strategies used to address these needs, and other adjunct information that would contribute to the effectiveness of the group.

GOALS, OBJECTIVES, STRATEGIES

Group goals should be consistent with individual goals so that all members can feel that they have a personal stake in making the group work. The leader should have this step in the planning process even though it will also be part of the first group session where members are asked for suggested group goals consistent with their individual ones.

Objectives and strategies are easier to develop after goals have been established. These are tentative at this point because the group as a whole has not accepted them as working goals. It would be unusual for the leader to be very off base in defining goals, but the group may have differing priorities for goals, which may lead to altering objectives and strategies. What is expected to be accomplished for each session, and what are the suggested strategies? It is also a good idea to list materials and supplies needed.

GROUP RULES

Every group develops overt and covert rules. These govern behavior in the group and specify what can and cannot be done. Some basic rules can be set by the leader, with others contributed by members. Rules suggested by the leader should be few in number and should consist of only those necessary for order in the group. Leaders should not forget that, although they can set rules, unless members commit to the rules they are most likely to be ignored. Some suggested rules are: attending each session on time; no food, drink or chewing gum; no hitting, fighting or physical violence; be an active participant; and maintain confidentiality.

EVALUATION OF GROUP

Leaders will find it personally and professionally useful to evaluate their groups. Some sort of evaluation should take place for every group conducted. Perceptions of group members, behavioral changes, what worked, what didn't work, what needs to be rethought or modified are possible topics for evaluation. The primary item is to what extent were goals accomplished. A truthful answer can point out successes, need for more narrowly focused goals, better specification of goals, the effectiveness of the mix of group and individual goals, and so forth. Seeing the results of evaluation is one way to help improve your groups.

SUGGESTED MODEL FOR GROUP SESSIONS

There are several basic assumptions for this suggested model; the focus for groups will be primarily process with content of lesser importance, groups will be brief (5–10 sessions), and the leader will understand the importance of using theory, process, and resources of the group to help individuals in the group. Techniques are used to enhance process and are not ends in and of themselves.

Assuming the leader has done all of the pre-preparation activities and planning for the group, he/she is ready to begin. The suggested procedures are designed for all groups no matter how experienced members are. They may take more time to accomplish with novice group members, but should not be neglected because members have participated in them before. Each group is different; however, certain basic needs have to be addressed. Members are always concerned about safety needs and how they will be met, their role in the group, expectations for and of members, and how their individual needs and goals can be met. Failure to address these concerns means the group does not progress adequately. Some are addressed directly, others are more hidden and are addressed indirectly.

It is difficult to prioritize the following procedures, as all are important but may have differing degrees of importance for each group. They are presented in an order that may be useful for deciding what to do in a session, for example, clarifying goals first, then addressing safety needs. However, the order is easily adjusted to suit needs of the group.

PROCEDURE(S) FOR GROUP SESSIONS

Beginning Session(s)

Get acquainted. Although group members may know each other, it is necessary that they develop a knowledge of each other as a group member so that connectedness and bonding can take place. A get-acquainted exercise is useful to help focus on another dimension of group members. Select an exercise that is nonthreatening, that all can participate in easily, and that is short and focuses on some part of the individual that may not be known to other members or the leader. An example is a drawing exercise that is easily done and can meet these conditions.

— Draw something you do well.
— Draw a symbol for what your name means to you.
— Draw something or a symbol for what makes you happy.
— Select a picture that represents you. (The leader should have a box of pictures cut from magazines. Pictures of people, flowers, scenes, animals, etc.)

One possible outcome may be a better understanding of how the child sees him/herself and how he/she wishes to be perceived by others.

Integrate group and individual goals and obtain group consensus. One process for doing this is to have each member first state what he/she would like to accomplish on a personal basis in the group. After each has stated a personal goal, try to tie them together into one or two possible goals. Ask members to suggest group goals that take into consideration what individual members have said. After all have had an opportunity for input, state what has emerged, ask if it is correct, and get agreement from members that these are acceptable group goals. Goals are end products and should be stated as such. It may be helpful to write suggestions on the board or posted paper.

This process can help clarify goals and get members' commitment to work on them. Another outcome is that members feel more a part of the decision-making process. Goals have not been imposed and all have contributed to them.

Openly address safety needs. Trust and cohesion occur when group members feel safe in the group. Safety in the group is best addressed directly, even though needs for safety may not be directly known to the individual. Learning to trust is a function of several factors including past experiences. Children, in many instances, are not fully aware of their past experiences and cannot be expected to understand the impact of these experiences on them. The group leader will probably have only minimal knowledge of members' past experiences and will not be able to anticipate the extent and level of safety needs. However, the presence of safety needs can always be anticipated.

One way of addressing safety needs openly is to ask members what will make them feel safe in the group. What behaviors make them feel less safe or trusting? What can the leader and members do to promote feelings of safety and trust. From this discussion the necessity for rules can be agreed upon, leading to setting rules for the group. Members should suggest rules first with the leader having input last. Go over the list and combine and/or modify suggestions to be reasonable and capable of being accomplished.

One rule and need that usually emerges is confidentiality. At this point the leader can describe what can and cannot be discussed outside the group. For a more specific discussion on communicating this to members, refer to the discussion in this chapter on pre-preparation for group.

Another concern that relates to safety needs is self-disclosure. The leader can emphasize that members have the freedom to decide when and how much to disclose. In order to reinforce the control over self-disclosure, the leader has to limit probing and/or rhetorical questioning.

Building on strengths. Most everyone is painfully aware of personal faults and weaknesses and can easily name most of them. Most also find it difficult to talk about strengths. Yet one of the most effective ways of building confidence is to emphasize strengths instead of remediating weaknesses. Group leaders can facilitate willingness to commit to working in the group by focusing on strengths and pointing out the positive side of characteristics that children bring up as faults. This is not to say that unacceptable behaviors are to be perceived positively. They are not. What is expected is that the leader's attitude, which is communicated to members, is one of perceiving, as much as possible, that which is positive.

For example, someone may be criticized for daydreaming. Assuming this behavior is not excessive and disturbing but only annoying, a strength may be that he/she can explore possibilities, is creative or likes to ponder in detail. Embedded in many faults or criticisms is a strength. Turn it around and make the child feel less flawed.

Identify support systems. Help group members identify those people to whom they can go for support. Who will listen to them, try to understand, and encourage them in their growth and development. Members of support systems can be parents, siblings, neighbors, teachers, and so on. Often people are not consciously aware of just how strong or weak their support system is. The group can serve as a support system for a short period of time, but over the long haul, others are needed.

Members can also become aware of what they give to others as a part of their support system. Mutual support is desirable and children are not often made aware of what they can or do contribute to others.

Empower group members. Give responsibility for who they are and what they can become to group members. While genetics, environment, and previous experiences all contribute to the development of the individual, some responsibility for what they do with these background characteristics belongs to the individual. Children can and should assume some responsibility for their behavior in order not to feel helpless. By empowering group members, the leader indicates confidence in their ability. This confidence expressed by the leader contributes to the development of self-esteem, self-confidence, and self-liking.

Most of these tasks can be accomplished in the first session. Some topics may need more discussion than others when members are novices. After participating in several groups, they are usually better able to clarify their goals, identify safety needs, understand the need for a support system, and have confidence in their ability to appropriately self-disclose. Even when tasks take more than one session, they can be addressed in a little more time, leaving other sessions for working and termination.

Working Sessions

Working sessions should be planned to meet specific issues/concerns for members, for example, dealing with loss. The group leader may decide to use direct strategies such as talking about the concern/issue, or may use indirect strategies, or a combination of the two. Some ideas for indirect techniques and strategies are discussed in detail in Chapters 6 and 7.

Termination

Planning for termination begins almost immediately, even though it is not verbalized directly. Knowing that there is a specific time frame means that there is conscious awareness that it will end.

Termination should not be ignored, and should not be abrupt or disruptive. It should be explored with awareness that this is an ending of something that will never be again. It is too valuable an experience to discount or to have its ending taken lightly. Teaching how to terminate relationships such as those developed for the group setting, but doing so in such a manner as to preserve the relationships in other settings, is a valuable learning exercise.

The leader should note how many sessions are left each time, for example, we have three sessions left, and may ask members how they think the time could be used productively. Termination should begin gradually by devoting a few minutes near the end of the last two or three sessions to discussing what and how to end the group. The leader can point out that there are feelings connected with termination and that members need to be aware of just what feelings are aroused in them associated with ending the group.

Enough time should be allotted for members to adequately express and resolve feelings connected with termination. The leader needs to understand his/her own issues with termination so that the process with group termination is not truncated because of coun-tertransference issues. While it is reasonable to want memories of the group to be pleasant, and closing on a happy note is desirable, ensuring that these are the only emotions felt may say more about the leader's needs than group members'.

Allow and encourage members to express and explore conflict-ing feelings about termination. They may enjoy the sessions but want to also do something else. Being able to express these feelings and having them heard and understood help alleviate feelings of guilt. Learning to adequately deal with conflicting feelings is a positive step. All too often people feel guilty about having conflict-ing feelings about someone, something, or a situation because they are told or made to feel that they are wrong for having these feelings. People are not wrong or bad for having these feelings, they just have them. Learning to accept these parts of self is healthy.

Having some closing experience helps to give termination a ritualistic feeling. There is a rite and official ending. This experi-ence should provide for each member to contribute in some way, but should not be a social event. Save the social event for after official termination. Some group leaders make what I consider to be a mistake by having a party for the closing experience. Members leave with a happy, pleasant experience, but there are usually unresolved feelings around ending the group that are not addressed. It is much better to do both, terminate and have a social event.

6

Art and Fairy Tales

Counselors and other therapists who work with children and adolescents continually seek ways to help them translate their experiences so that they can be understood, and appropriate interventions made. One way, using fairy tales, aids in identifying object-relations and existential issues that are primary for the individual. Using the described process in group counseling promotes the therapeutic factors described by Yalom (1985) of universality, instillation of hope, the corrective recapitulation of the primary family group, and existential factors.

Children, traumatized adolescents and adults, and people of all ages with low verbal skills usually find it difficult to communicate adequately by using words. Counselors have to rely on a process to encourage expressions of experiences through indirect means that do not rely on an ability to use language. Games, sand trays, dolls, clay, art and fairy tales are examples of indirect means of translating primary process into words.

FAIRY TALES

Review of Literature

A fairy tale is defined in *The American Heritage Dictionary* (1976) as "a fanciful tale of legendary deeds and romance usually intended to please children."

Bettelheim (1975), in *The Uses of Enchantment*, points out that

> in order to master the psychological problems of growing up—overcoming narcissistic disappointments, oedipal dilemmas, sibling rivalries; becoming able to relinquish childhood dependencies; gaining a feeling of selfhood and self-worth, and a sense of moral obligation—a child needs to understand what is going on within his (her) conscious self so that he (she) can also cope with that which goes on in his (her) unconscious. (parentheses mine)

He feels that fairy tales provide a unique mechanism whereby the child can fit unconscious content into conscious fantasies, and this will enable him/her to deal with that content. The basic message of fairy tales is that "a struggle against severe difficulties in life is unavoidable, is an intrinsic part of human existence—but that if one does not shy away, but steadfastly meets unexpected and often unjust hardships, one masters all obstacles and at the end emerges victorious" (Bettelheim, 1975, p. 8).

Fairy tales present existential dilemmas directly and briefly. All situations, characters, and actions are simplified and unambiguous. Polarizations are characteristic of fairy tales just as they prevail in children's thinking.

Some other perspectives on the usefulness of fairy tales in therapy follow. Thiessen (1985) used fairy tales to bypass conscious control and stimulate the client to participate in needed changes. He found that fairy tales directed attention to solutions of psychological conflict by metaphors of fairy tales matched to problems. Thiessen (1988) also proposes that life values such as honesty, loyalty, self-control, and caring, are implanted through fairy tales. They become a motivator for good or bad behavior and promote a sense of well-being. Davies (1988) found that fairy tales can be employed as extended metaphors which function as vehicles for reframing. Lehmkuhl (1988) used fairy tales as clarification of inner and socially based human problems, and to assist in integrating aspects of personality, including the unconscious. Heuscher (1989) points out the usefulness of fairy tales in addressing existential issues when she says, "genuine fairy tales point to basic aspects of human existence, to existential possibilities, to the meaning of life."

A variety of problems and populations appear to respond to the therapeutic use of fairy tales: death education for children (Ryerson, 1977), children and abuse (Belcher, 1983), behavioral problems (Crain, 1983), and eating disorders (Hill, 1992).

An Object-Relations Perspective

Margaret Mahler (1968) defined therapy as being based on the developmental needs of the patient. The process of therapy enables the reexperiencing of early stages of development leading to higher levels of object relationships. As an example, she theorizes that borderline and narcissistic disorders occur when the developmental process through the separation-individuation phase is disturbed or not completed. Symptoms such as omnipotence, splitting, and grandiosity are behaviors associated with disruptions in this phase.

Bettelheim (1975) points to the role of fairy tales in fulfilling the child's needs in the developmental process. They entertain, arouse a child's curiosity, explore life's difficulties, address a wide range of feelings, and offer solutions that are clear and direct. Most of all they provide hope to a child that he/she can surmount difficulties during psychological growth and development constructively.

Metaphors

Metaphors serve an important purpose in helping children decipher feelings and attitudes concerning self and others. Metaphors are also used to help children grow, understand, develop ego-strength and well-being, and allow them to derive unique and personal meaning—to "grasp intuitively multiple messages" (Thiessen, 1988). Another perspective on the importance and relevance of metaphors within fairy tales is given by Walker and Lunz (1976) who perceive archetypal material as "interrelated symbols of unconscious psychic processes relating to self" (p. 95).

Although metaphors are used on an individual basis, generalized meanings can still be given to the various metaphors, allowing a better understanding of existential and object-relations meaning within the fairy tales. Metaphors aid the child in understanding concepts such as splitting and existential meaning of life and self within the world. For example, stepmothers are characters found in many fairy tales, and their purpose can be interpreted in several ways: (1) protecting both mother and child from the child's anger, (2) bonding mother and child by showing the negative side of any mother substitute (Radomisli, 1981), (3) showing a mother who does not desire to be a mother (Theissen, 1988), (4) providing the split between the "good" and "bad" mother, thereby helping the child to integrate the two (Cashdan, 1988), (5) helping the child preserve the image of the "good" mother without contaminating that "good" with the "bad" mother (Bettelheim, 1975), and (6) splitting the "good" mother from the "bad" mother, thus allowing the child to separate (Berman, 1991) during the rapprochement and object-constancy phases (Shapiro, 1968).

Existential Factors

Yalom (1985) includes five items as defining existential factors: "Recognizing that life is at times unfair and unjust, recognizing that ultimately there is no escape from some of life's pain and from death, recognizing that no matter how close I get to other people, I must still face life alone, facing the basic issues of my life and death, and thus living my life more honestly and being less caught up in trivialities, and learning that I must take responsibility for the way I live my life no matter how much guidance and support I get from others."

Two examples of how fairy tales deal with existential factors follow. Death anxiety is dealt with in fairy tales by "If they have not died, they are still alive"; or "They lived happily ever after." The sting of realizing one's own death can be endured by forming a truly satisfying bond with another. If we try to escape our separation or death anxiety by holding on desperately to another, we may be cast out.

The existential factor of isolation is exemplified by the hero who proceeds alone for a while, may feel like an outcast, abandoned in the world, groping in the dark. However, he/she is guided step-by-step, given help, and ultimately establishes meaningful relationships with the world around him/her.

Fairy Tales versus Myths

Why not use myths? Myths are defined (*American Heritage Dictionary*, 1976) as a traditional story originating in a preliterate society dealing with supernatural beings, ancestors or heroes that serve as primordial types in a primitive view of the world. "Myths bring the unknown into relation with the known" (Cecil M. Bowra, in *The American Heritage Dictionary*, 1976).

Myths, more often than fairy tales, present the culture's hero as someone to be emulated, a role model. The theme is presented majestically, has a spiritual force, and the divine is involved via superhuman heroes.

Both fairy tales and myths personify and illustrate inner conflicts, but most fairy tales make no demands on the listener; rather, they subtly suggest how conflicts can be solved and what the next steps in development might be. Both use symbols to express unconscious material. Both have exemplary figures and situations. Both have miraculous events.

Myths differ from fairy tales in some important ways. In a myth it could only have happened to this being and endings are almost always tragic. Myths are pessimistic while fairy tales are optimistic; myths involve superego demands in conflict with id-motivated action, together with the self-preserving desires of the ego; the central figure experience a transfiguration into heaven; and the hero and other characters have names.

Fairy tales present the possibility that anyone could have the experience, the endings are positive and constructive, the characters live happily every after on earth (a happy but ordinary existence).

The problems presented in fairy tales are ordinary—jealousy, sibling rivalry, being thought incompetent by parents. Solutions are worked out on earth. Few characters have a name, for example, "A little red cap suited her so well that she was always called Little Red Cap," or generic names are used.

> Fairy tales are told for entertainment. You've got to distinguish between the myths that have to do with the serious matter of living life in terms of the order of society and of nature, and stories with some of those same motifs that are told for entertainment. Fairy tales are for children. Many of the Grimm tales represent the little girl who is stuck (at a developmental level). All of these dragon killings and threshold crossings have to do with getting past being stuck. (Campbell, 1988)

Procedure and Materials

Distribute paper and drawing implements before beginning the story. Ask group members to get comfortable, close their eyes and listen to the story. Read a fairy tale. When you are finished, tell them to open their eyes and draw two scenes from the story. After they finish, ask them to title the scenes and let each member share his/her work in the group. Do no interpretations, just nonjudgmental comments. Collect the drawings for your analysis.

Fairy tales that will be used in the analysis procedure that follows should be from the Grimm Brothers' version. These are the ones analyzed by Bettelheim and the object-relations and existential issues symbols come from that version.

Another consideration is the choice of a fairy tale. Following is a list of fairy tales with suggested themes (Table 6.1). Select the story that best fits the needs of the group as you perceive them to be. A checklist for symbols in "Hansel and Gretel" is in the

Table 6.1
Suggested Themes in Fairy Tales

Fairy Tale	Theme(s)
The Three Little Pigs	Pleasure versus Reality Principles
The Queen Bee	Resolving conflicting aspects of personality
Brother and Sister	Bringing destructive tendencies (id) under control by altruism (superego)
Hansel and Gretel	Separation, individuation, a female rescuer
Little Red Riding Hood	Struggle with pubertal problems, threat of being devoured
Jack and the Beanstalk	Struggle to achieve maturity, conflict between father and son
Snow White	Conflicts between mother and daughter, successful completion of developmental levels, and adolescence. Focus on parenting
Goldilocks and the Three Bears	The search for identity
The Sleeping Beauty	Prepuberty and sexual awakening
Cinderella	Sibling rivalry, steps in personality development leading to self-fulfillment, sexual awakening

appendices. These checklists are derived from the analyses by Bettelheim (1975). Children, adolescents and adults can enjoy hearing a fairy tale and the drawing afterwards. Choices for scenes drawn are personal and appear to tune in to that which is important for the individual at that time. Even children of the same age group will have differing personal issues and these differences can emerge in their drawings. Selection of a fairy tale is important but not crucial, as each member personalizes it for him or herself.

To derive checklists for a simple analysis of scenes drawn after hearing a fairy tale, you can consult *The Uses of Enchantment* by Bruno Bettleheim (1975). Many other books are published on symbolism and should be read.

ART TECHNIQUES

"Fantasies, dreams, and play, are the organizers of our primary process, contain the raw affects of our inner experiences" (Robbins, 1980). The counselor or therapist who can elicit and understand what emerges when expressive techniques are used has a guide to the inner and outer world of the client and some clues on the psychic development. Much of this material is not readily available to the individual and because it isn't, it takes considerable time before it emerges into awareness and can be verbalized.

Another factor may be the inability to adequately verbalize relevant material. Children may not have the words or ability to verbally express complex concepts so that others can understand what they mean or are experiencing. Indirect means of eliciting relevant material can be very useful, and techniques that use art, play, imagery, music, drama, literature, and so on can play a role in helping the individual, the group, and the leader to deeper and better understandings.

Art techniques, like all others, are best used to accomplish a clear objective. That is, the group leader should be clear in his/her mind about just what is to be gained by group members from use of the technique. In addition, selection of an appropriate technique, exercise, and media is dependent on the purpose.

Art is also a useful adjunct to other expressive techniques such as imagery, fairy tales, and music. It is especially useful in these combinations in groups as it allows for individual expression untainted by contributions or thoughts of others. The use of art in combination with other expressive techniques is covered in those sections. The following discussion will focus on using art only.

Art-Focused Techniques

Art psychotherapists are trained to interpret art products focusing on latent meanings and symbolism in the product. Art therapists using the psychoanalytic approach interpret the product in terms of unconscious themes, transferences, sublimations, and catharsis.

Art can also be used therapeutically to provide an opportunity for freer expression of self, feelings, and thoughts. When used this way, no interpretations are made by others, only by the individual him/herself. The focus is on expressing, not interpreting, although significant and deep understandings may emerge. This approach to using art is the one emphasized in this book. What follows assumes the group leader is not trained to be an art therapist but has an interest in use of art techniques and has had some exposure to them.

Group Members

Many people are uncomfortable with art techniques because they feel or have been told that they have no talent. This is less so with children, but it is not uncommon to encounter this attitude in children. When planning to use an art technique, the leader should be sensitive to these possible attitudes.

Group members may also seek to be "right" and may need encouragement to free themselves from the injunction. Be patient, give encouragement, but do not label or evaluate the products. It may be easy not to criticize the product but care must also be taken not to praise some products. Learn to limit comments to "interesting," "it's coming along" or any other neutral comment. It's best not to say anything that could be perceived as a value judgment.

Materials and Supplies for Drawing

The setting should be conducive to the art experience. There should be enough room for each member to work in comfort, and adequate materials. The art exercise should be selected for a particular purpose and the same is true for your choice of media. Most drawing exercises can be accomplished by using graphite pencils, charcoal, chalk pastels, oil pastels, felt-tip watercolors, or crayons. Each has specific qualities that contribute to the pleasure derived from doing art.

Pencils have the advantage of being readily available and come with degrees of soft to hard lead. Soft lead doesn't take much physical pressure to make marks but it smears easily. Children are very sensitive to "messing up" and may get upset when their drawing is smudged.

Charcoal is easy to grasp, makes marks easily, can be smudged for shading effects, and can be used as a stick or with fingers to make designs. It is very messy and cleanup materials should be kept right at hand.

Chalk pastels come in colors that are easily transferred to paper. Color can be layered, mixed, or smudged. As with charcoal, cleanup materials are necessary.

Oil pastels glide easily on paper. They have easy applicability, like chalk pastels, but also have the added advantage of being less messy. Colors are brilliant and can be mixed, overlaid, rubbed, or smudged.

Felt-tip watercolors are available at very little cost in a vast array of colors. They can be secured in either fine line or broad tips, clean up easily, and are easily applied to paper. Some are even scented.

Crayons are also available in a vast array of colors. They are not messy but there is some resistance when applied to paper. They do not glide easily as do felt tips, chalk pastels, and oil pastels. Use crayons if other materials are not available in supplies sufficient for each member to have what he or she needs.

There are other media that can provide a very satisfying experience. However, the emphasis is on producing a product and less on the experience—which is the primary reason for doing the exercise.

A word about paper. Provide paper in large enough quantities so group members can make mistakes. The sheets should be large enough for expression, about 18" x 24." Newsprint is adequate and has the advantage of being less costly than other kinds of paper. Paper should be neutral in color and, for that reason, colored construction paper is not recommended for drawing activities.

Materials and Supplies for Collages

Papers such as tissue, construction, crepe, kraft, and poster board, magazine illustrations, and yarn, glue, sticks, felt tips, crayons, or oil pastels are materials that can be used to make collages. Materials for collages should be easily worked with and capable of a wide range of expressiveness.

Materials and Supplies for Other Art Exercises

Examples of other art exercises are sculpting, using photographs, constructing murals and the paper bag exercise.

Sculpting can be focused on many different topics or concerns. Group members can sculpt a symbol for a concept such as love, their family, how they perceive themselves, or any abstraction. Materials for children should be easy to clean up and manipulate. Either a nonhardening compound such as Playdoh or an air drying compound such as Sculpy could be used if it were important to preserve the product.

Photographs can be used in a variety of ways. Group members can make a collage that depicts them through the years; take pictures of favorite people, places or things and describe their meanings to the group; or use photographs to prepare a display or book depicting themselves. There could even be a group collage.

A mural can be a group project. They must work as a team to plan and produce the mural. Subjects for a mural include perceptions of the group by the group members, the group members, feelings, expressions, and so on. Materials include cut paper shapes, felt tips, oil pastels, crayons, found objects, photographs, magazine cutouts, and so on.

The paper bag exercise is an expanded collage. Symbols of self that are easily talked about are pasted on the outside of the bag. Symbols of self that are not easily revealed (or values) are put inside. The outside is shared in the group and any of the inside the member wants to reveal. However, *none* of the inside needs to be revealed. Materials are magazines for clipping symbols of self, glue sticks, and felt-tip markers. Plain brown or white paper bags of any size can be used as can clasp envelopes 8" x 11" or larger. This exercise can be a homework assignment or completed during a session.

Examples of Drawing Exercises

- Name card with a drawing of something about self. The instructions given should be sufficiently vague so members can draw anything. The purposes are to introduce members and begin to convey an openness and acceptance.

- Symbols for emotions. One emotion can be the focus or several can be explored. For example, draw a symbol for love. Materials needed are paper and either pencils, charcoal, chalk pastels, oil pastels, felt tips, or crayons.

- Draw a dream. Draw a fragment, a scene, or whatever is remembered. If only feelings are remembered, draw these. Sharing the pictures in the group is important.

- Draw your physical self, your emotional or feeling self, and your fun or playful self.

- Draw a coat of arms. Provide a drawn shield on paper divided into six sections. Ask group members to draw a symbol in each section that describes them. Section one: an achievement of which they are proud. Section two: something they do well or a talent they have. Section three: something they wish they could do well. Section four: something material they want. Section five: something they like. Section six: their favorite color and flower.

Art Ideas from the Literature

The literature contains hundreds of ideas for art activities that are useful in therapy. Most can be adapted for use with all age clients, and many are appropriate for group therapy. Following are several art techniques described in the literature as used with children. The description usually includes the problem/issue or concern for the client but they can be applied or modified for most conditions.

Katz (1987) describes using photocollage as a therapeutic technique with a group of eight-year-old girls experiencing rapid mood shifts and poor social relationships. The children had been identified as having academic underachievement and poor adaptability to the classroom. Group consisted of 12 sessions focused on construction of a photocollage during each session. The subject of each photocollage was derived from assessing the needs of the group members and identified behaviors. Materials for collages were pictures from magazines, photographs, construction paper, and felt tips. After constructing a collage on the topic for the day, members discussed their products and personal associations were made.

Ferrara (1991) reports on art therapy with a disturbed, hearing-impaired Cree boy. Because of low verbalization skills, art was introduced as a means of expressing feelings. Each session was begun with drawing a picture. The instructions were to draw anything he wanted to. The picture was discussed with the client, making the associations for each symbol in the picture. The therapist collected the pictures and began to analyze recurring symbols and the associations made by the child. Through art, the child became less anxious and behavior improved.

Cohene and Cohene (1989) described art therapy with deaf children. Techniques included drawing with the eyes closed, drawing with the nondominant hand, and a joint drawing between the client and the therapist.

Sourkes (1991) illustrates the use of a structured mandala with pediatric oncology patients and their siblings. The purpose of the structured mandala is to help the children focus and express feelings around their illness and the changed relationships. There are six parts to the strategy: definition of the topic, guided visualization, development of a set of feelings, color-feeling match, proportion of colors-feelings, and associations.

The topic for the mandala is selected together with the child or children. Guided visualization begins with the child being asked to visualize an event around the topic (for Sourkes's clients it was when they found out they had cancer). The therapist or leader presents a set (8–10) of feelings that are commonly attributed to the experience. Feelings can be those selected by the client or those that emerged from the guided visualization. After the child opens his/her eyes, a piece of paper is presented with a circle drawn on it and a set of colors, such as crayons. The child is directed to choose a color to match each feeling and color in a part of a circle. If the named feeling appears big to the child, he/she is instructed to make the portion of the circle with that color big. If the feeling is not big, then the space used is small. If the child had feelings around the visualization that were not mentioned, he/she is to include these also. Sourkes (1991) notes that the list of feelings should be no more than eight and that the child should be provided at least that number of colors.

We like to think of disasters as rare; however, they have become less rare and there is a need to anticipate what could be done, in the event of a disaster, to help the children. Klingman, Koenigsfeld, and Markman (1987) describe what was done for an elementary school where several children attending the school died in a disaster. A creativity room was set up where children could use materials to express their feelings. Children were free to come and go at will to the room and to make anything they wished. Materials provided included scrap paper, old magazines, construction paper, cardboard, crayons, oil pastels, gouache paints, colored chalk, glue, scissors, paintbrushes, and paper clips of various sizes. While there was some crisis counseling for the children, personnel was limited and the creativity room was felt to be a resource whereby those who felt a need to express some feelings around the disaster could do so whenever they wished, without having to wait their turn with the professional.

7

Drama, Music, and Imagery

Other expressive techniques to aid group process with children are discussed in this chapter. Each, as do art and fairy tales, has the potential for being a therapeutic focus for the group. However, when used this way the group leader has the responsibility to become fully trained in the technique of therapy. The uses discussed herein are proposed as techniques to be used in the framework of some other theoretical approach. Drama, music, and imagery are also indirect approaches that can facilitate expressions of vague, complex, and/or difficult thoughts and feelings.

DRAMA

Dramatic techniques discussed include puppets, role-play, and mime, all of which have been used successfully in classrooms for teaching purposes. Children like acting and seeing others act and can be very spontaneous. Guidance is needed to help them become focused on themselves and to encourage expressions of thoughts and feelings. The group leader needs to be tuned in and highly aware of the meanings that underlie the performance, so that appropriate interventions can be made.

When dramatic techniques are used in a group setting, the performance also has an impact on the audience. The impact may take the form of "coattailing" when group member(s) use what is being expressed to access their own issues. Or, the impact may be empathic, sensing what the other is feeling. Or, the impact may create universality, becoming aware of one's own situation being similar. It is the group leader's responsibility to stay in touch with all group members and to provide an opportunity for them to openly express the impact of the performance on them.

Dramatherapy

Mosley (1988) points out that dramatherapy can help children to gain deeper insight and understanding of their behavior, enhance self-understanding, develop empathy for others' points of view, and confront them with the consequence of their actions. She goes on to describe how this form of therapeutic role-play is used with children in a school setting.

The goal was to help children with behavior problems become more responsible for their behavior. Children participated in weekly group sessions where individual target goals for behavior change are assessed and discussed. Prior to being in the group each child had, together with the group leader, set goals and agreed to a contract for behavior changes. If the child has not been able to meet his/her target goals for the week, the situations or ongoing conflicts that interfere with attaining the goal form the basis for role-play.

Sessions begin with a goal checkup. The basis for a role-play is established and entered into starting with a warm-up game. Ice breakers, tension relievers, and other short activities are generally used to bring members into the here and now and have them concentrated on the group. The role-play action phase is accomplished in several ways: having the child play all actors in the conflict or situation, having the child try different ways of responding in the situation, or combining art and drama. There is always a period for discussion after the role-play.

Dunne (1988) describes dramatherapy as being grounded in the creative process. She feels that this approach allows the client to be somewhat disassociated from the material and creates a safe environment to express feelings. It contrasts with psychodrama, according to Dunne, as "psychodrama is direct and confrontive dealing primarily with actual scenes in an individual's life." Dunne goes on to describe dramatherapy techniques used with disturbed children and adolescents.

The techniques described are structured exercises that include narrative pantomime, creative movement, and guided imagery. Stage one consists of a warm-up with hypothetical problem-solving situations, ongoing drama, and pictorial dramatization. Stage two focuses on dramatic reenactment. Discussion or processing occurs in stage three along with closure.

Stage one has the goals of clarifying issues and exploration of feelings. Structured activities are generally used as the guidance provided by structure promotes feelings of safety in the beginning. By using narrative pantomime the therapist sets the stage and develops the narrative for the role-play. The child does the role-play under the direction of the leader. Creative movement is used when children have difficulty with verbal expressiveness. Movement is used to express inner selves and feelings and music may or may not be used. Guided imagery works well as a warm-up for inhibited children. More structured cues are used to develop the imagery.

Stage two is dramatic reenactment of that which is important to the child, the conflict, relationship, situation, event, and so forth. Dunne (1988) describes ongoing drama as "improvisational drama based on a subject of interest to the participant or group continuing from session to session." The focus of the drama may be real or imaginary. Hypothetical problem-solving situations emerge out of unresolved conflicts. The leader suggests several ideas for hypothetical scenes that deal with similar problems. After the child selects one, he/she acts out the scene improvisationally with the leader participating, if necessary. Role reversal is also used with problem-solving situations.

Another approach asks group members to draw a picture of an important moment, person, conflict, or fantasy in pictorial dramatization. They then act out short, improvisational scenes based on the picture. From the drama comes more information on how the child perceives him/herself and significant inner feelings that may not be in the child's awareness or have not been expressed openly.

It is very important to have appropriate closure. This is the stage where insight occurs and integration can take place. Dunne (1988) suggests that this can be accomplished verbally or by use of further dramatic techniques. Making specific links to the person's life, verbalizing what emerged, and helping to clarify are all tasks that are a part of stage three.

Mosley (1988, 1991) describes the functioning of a dramatherapy peer support group within a comprehensive school. The group was developed in response to teachers' concerns about problem behaviors of some children. The behaviors that were of concern fell into three categories: lack of self-control, such as interfering with others while they are working; hostile behavior, such as outbursts of aggression; and withdrawn behavior, such as isolation on the playground. In preparing for group sessions, children developed a contract for the group that specified goals and ground rules. The format for each session was preliminary discussion, warm-up, action, and reflection.

The preliminary discussion phase performs two purposes: to allow each member an opportunity to have a personal goal check-up and to set the focus for the remainder of the session. Members recount their week with an emphasis on continuing areas of concern. These concerns provide the topic for the drama that follows.

During the warm-up phase any of a variety of approaches are used: games, relaxation, brainstorming, and so on. Activity during the warm-up should be related to the theme that emerged during the discussion phase and provide for more concentration on the topic. What happens during warm-up also helps the leader assess the members' readiness to move on.

The action phase involves the dramatization of interests, dilemmas, or conflicts. The group member can assume all of the roles or other members can play some parts in the drama. Mosley (1988, 1991) does not emphasize emotional involvement but focuses more on cognitive understanding in order to develop rational insights.

Mosley (1988, 1991) uses the reflection phase as the calming-down period to bring the child back to the present and allow him/her to relinquish the role. Discussion of the experience aids in developing understandings.

Huddleston (1989) describes the use of drama with the elderly. While the goals were different for this group, some of the strategies used could also be used with children: play-making, role-play, mime, spontaneous scenes, paintings, pictures and photographs as stimuli, and literature such as poems and scenes from well-known plays.

Play-making refers to group members developing their own story or theme and then acting it out. Role-play is similar to that discussed elsewhere. Mime is used to help members develop a means of communication to facilitate relationships. It is also used to increase awareness of movement, such as how they use their bodies. Spontaneous scenes are developed from stimuli such as dreams, ambitions, wishes, everyday objects, and tools. Pictures and photographs are presented, and members are asked to act out what is happening in the picture, what is being said and done, and what is felt. Guided fantasies are developed from poems and scenes from well-known plays.

PROCEDURE FOR USING DRAMA TECHNIQUES

Warm-Up and Introduction

Each of the following techniques, puppets, role-play, and mime, should be implemented after the group has had more than one session. If any is used for the final session, it should be chosen and planned carefully for there will not be an opportunity for *this group* to adequately process intense feelings that may emerge. Processing adequately is crucial and, while individuals can be worked with after the group ends, this particular group will not continue to exist.

A brief warm-up is recommended before conducting exercises. This is the period when the purpose of the exercise is explained and the leader checks in with each group member to evaluate his/her readiness to participate. During this period the leader has an opportunity to determine if there is something more urgent and important that needs to be worked on before that which is planned. Needless to say, the exercise would be delayed if this were the case.

The warm-up period also allows group members to become more present-centered and better able to tune in to the group and to themselves. Most exercises produce best results when members are more fully in the here and now.

Some mechanisms for the warm-up period include relaxation with a focus on becoming aware of bodily sensations, having a go-around so each member can tell what he/she is feeling or is aware of at this time, or briefly relating some personal input relative to the purpose of the exercise.

Introduce the exercise by telling members the goal(s) and objective(s), directions for completing the exercise, what to do if they become anxious and want to stop participating, and how the exercise will be processed.

Puppets

There are numerous prepackaged puppets with exercises available for use by mental health professionals. They have been tested and found useful when working with children. They can be used as they are or modified for use with a particular group or purpose.

The group leader can also make some puppets for his/her particular use. These will have the advantage of being customized for a therapeutic purpose.

Another approach allows group members to make their own puppets. This way they have the fun and sense of accomplishment that accompanies constructing a puppet as well as their personal involvement in the product.

However, a more important part is the dramatic presentation using puppets. The stage for the presentation should be set by the leader who asks for a reenactment of a significant feeling, event, or situation. One, several, or all group members can participate in the "show."

Enough time should be allowed for processing the experience. Topics that could be explored are the associations or symbolism of the puppet(s), feelings during the performance, suggested other ways of behaving or communicating, and present feelings after the exercise.

Role-Play

Role-playing is usually used to help individuals develop a better understanding of themselves, of others, or for behavior rehearsal. Roles can be assumed by the individual him/herself or assumed by others with the individuals as a director/observer.

If the group leader feels that a role-play would be useful for the group, it can be suggested. Role-play should *never be imposed*. Introduce the idea and ask group members if they would like to try it. All too often a group leader will decide that role-playing would produce insight and proceeds to implement it. Members are put in the position of having to go along and participate or openly rebel. Most often there is passive resistance under these circumstances. That is, members participate but not much happens in a therapeutic sense. Insight and new learning or awarenesses do not emerge, and the leader becomes frustrated. Active participation allows insight, learning, and awarenesses to emerge and fosters the therapeutic environment. This is why it is so very important to get members' permission prior to role-play.

Role-plays are most useful when kept simple, that is, not too many actors/actresses and the event is simplified. If there is a point to be made, keep the role-play on that point. Remember, processing allows the group to expand on the point.

Before action begins, the member or members should set the scene. Identify participants (for young children, name tags, e.g., teacher, may be useful), describe the setting where the action is taking place (this helps bring it into the here and now), and briefly discuss the action. Group members not participating in the role-play are charged with observing and tuning in to their own feelings as the action unfolds.

Now, the stage is set and the action begins. The group leader should give few directions, encourage action, and be alert to when it should stop, that is, no more relevant data is forthcoming or will emerge.

There are several methods for role-playing that produce relevant material. Some are briefly described below.

- A group member agrees to explore an issue or concern in more depth and he/she plays all roles. Care must be taken to adequately describe the scene and identify participants. Try to limit roles to two or three, including the personal role being portrayed.
- In exploring an agreed-upon issue/concern, roles are assigned to other group members. The identified member should select members to play the various roles and the selection need not be gender specific. That is, one needn't be a female to play a female's role. The identified member can participate in the role-play *or* can direct and observe. Enough information should be provided for others to play their roles.
- Roles assumed could be different parts of self. For example, if a member is trying to make a decision, he/she could play all sides of the conflict.

Processing after the role-play should focus on feelings experienced in the different roles or by different participants. New learnings and insight may have emerged and participants must always be asked if that happened. Observers must also have an opportunity to relate their experiences during the role-play with an emphasis on personal experiencing.

Mime

Mime allows feelings, situations, and events to be acted out in pantomime. This is a nonverbal portrayal using gestures and body movement or positions to convey that which words are inadequate to communicate. This form of drama is particularly useful for anyone lacking verbal skills or who has trouble verbalizing complex thoughts or feelings.

Few props or materials are needed. Professional mimes use exaggerated makeup but that is not essential under these circumstances. Children could have fun designing their faces and the mime face could also provide clues as to what is going on for that person.

Some children may not have participated in pantomime and would have to be taught or shown. Letting a group member who knows how to do it is one way of teaching and also gives the group members a feeling of safety to risk trying one themselves.

MUSIC

When using music exercises, care must be taken not to let the music become an end in itself. Music should be used to evoke expressions of feelings that may have been repressed, suppressed, denied, and/or difficult to express. Music can also be used to help children become more aware of nuances as well as intense feelings. They can be taught to identify feelings using music.

Music can also be used in conjunction with other expressive therapeutic techniques, such as dance. However it is used, the purpose must be clearly understood and the music not become the purpose. Another way of saying this is to remember that the purpose is not music appreciation nor to evoke anything specific. Music is a vehicle or mechanism by which to access and express something personal and meaningful.

Selection of musical pieces is also important. When currently popular pieces are used, the session may become a social event or members may get caught up in the lyrics and/or words and forget the purpose. I like to separate words and lyrics by finding recordings of popular music without words. Words of songs can be used as poetry, which can be another expressive technique.

Classical music, jazz, and what is termed "soft rock" are categories of music that have selections or parts of pieces useful in groups to evoke emotional expression. It would probably be helpful to consult with a musician on selection. Describe what you are trying to evoke in group members and he/she can make suggestions. Whatever is chosen, the primary goals for the session and the group must be remembered.

Suggested exercises using music are:

- Play a short piece and have group members draw what was evoked. Scenes, feelings, symbols, colors, and so on are all appropriate. Each member must be given an opportunity to share what emerged for him/her.

- Play several short selections chosen to highlight different emotions. Members can identify or draw what emerged for them. Group processing of the experience is important.

- Music can form a scene for a mime. The nonverbal communication mirrors a message in the music, expands and enhances it. Group members can be made more aware of the many ways of communicating feelings. The leader should process what the experience was like for group members and for the mime.

IMAGERY

Visualizing is a very powerful technique. Through visualization individuals become aware of potentials, participate in behavior rehearsal, and develop greater self-awarenesses. One of the advantages of imagery is that the associations and symbols evoked are controlled by the individual. Even in guided imagery, cues are suggestions and the individual produces the images.

Always introduce an imagery exercise by explaining the purpose, what will be done, and ask permission from members. If there are any objections or reservations, substitute another exercise. Do not attempt to persuade or cajole in any way. Don't leave members out of the exercise by telling them they can keep their eyes open. After all, it is supposed to be a safe group experience.

If this is the first time a member or members have participated in an imagery exercise, explain the procedure thoroughly and try one of the suggested introductory exercises. Children may have to have several introductory exercises before engaging in a more focused one. On the other hand, many children are less resistant than many adults and can fully participate from the beginning.

In introducing an imagery exercise describe the purpose, procedure, and safeguards or control mechanisms. The purpose should be one of value to the group-as-a-whole. For example, if most or all members are having difficulty expressing an intense emotion, such as sadness or anger, an imagery exercise to facilitate expression would be appropriate. It would not be appropriate if only one or two members had difficulty. Other methods, such as drawing, role-play, mime, and so forth would be more useful. The leader should identify a group need or purpose before initiating an imagery exercise.

Describe the procedure in some detail, especially if this is their first experience with imagery. The basic procedure involves getting comfortable, closing eyes, relaxing, listening, and not editing or changing images. Group members could sit or lie on the floor for maximum comfort but sitting in a chair is acceptable also.

Some like to play background music. If it is used, turn it off when presenting cues as it may interfere with the process. For some members, getting comfortable and closing eyes can be facilitated with background music. For others, it is a nuisance, as they begin to focus on the music and not themselves.

Relaxation can be accomplished by tensing and relaxing muscle groups such as feet, legs. Too much relaxing and members may drift off or go to sleep. Either way, it defeats the purpose of the exercise.

Listening to the cues presented by the leader and allowing images to emerge may be difficult at first for some members. Explain that colors, feelings, or fragments may emerge and are acceptable. Anything produced is valuable and can be worked with productively. It is very important to accept whatever emerges and not try to edit or change it in any way.

Safeguards or controls against anxious feelings or uncomfortable feelings must be emphasized. Members can stop the imaging at any time by opening their eyes and *must* be given permission to do so when explaining the procedure.

Before beginning the exercise, provide or decide on a mechanism for reporting the individual experiencing. Drawing what emerged is useful with children as it keeps the personal experience intact. Verbally describing the experience runs the risk of confabulation as members begin to incorporate what others report. Drawing also allows for reporting vagueness, colors, and the like.

The final steps are reporting in the group and processing the experience. Give time constraints. It is evident that imagery exercises used in brief groups must be short in order to allow time for the final steps. It is possible to carry over into the next session;

however, carryover is not recommended, as the impact and intensity of the exercise are lost when there is a hiatus.

Some introductory exercises follow. All cues should be presented slowly with pauses. Give enough time for an image to emerge.

- Visualize or image a flower. What kind of flower is it? What color? Note the shape and smell (if any). When you are ready, open your eyes and draw the flower.

- Visualize a room you like. What is in the room? Furniture, people, pets, and so on. What kind of feeling does the room give you? Are you in the room? When you are ready, open your eyes and draw the room.

- Visualize or image sadness. Note the shape, size, and color(s). When you are ready, open your eyes and draw what you saw. Any emotion can be the focus, for example, happiness, anger, love, and so on.

After group members become comfortable with imagery, more complex and longer exercises can be used. Fantasy trips are not recommended as they are threatening to some groups and, most important, are too long and complex to adequately complete in the allotted time. Select brief exercises with a few focused cues relevant to the group. Some examples follow.

- Visualize or image a place of peace. Not where it is, what's included, colors, sounds, smells, and so on. What feelings are aroused? When you are ready, come back to the room, open your eyes, and draw your place of peace.

- Visualize a meadow (field) where you are walking on a pretty day. What's in the meadow? Note colors, smells, sounds, feelings. As you walk through the meadow you see someone coming toward you. It's someone with whom you have a conflict. What do you do? How do you feel? When you are ready, come back to the room, open your eyes, and record or draw the experience. *Note.* Processing should focus on characteristic ways of behaving in conflict situations.

- Visualize or image yourself as someone who is meeting you for the first time would see you. (Pause) Now, image yourself as your friends see you. (Pause) Finally, image yourself as you see you. When you are ready, come back to the room, open your eyes and draw your 3 "selves."

There are numerous references that have suggested imagery exercises. Group leaders can also create their own by reflecting on what symbols or associations they wish to elicit from group members. Examples are: climbing a mountain (symbolic of completing a difficult undertaking); building a house (developing a relationship); and receiving or giving gifts (inner resources). Any of these can be made more elaborate and deep.

Imagery exercises are fun as well as productive. Following suggested guidelines and procedures facilitates exercises that can foster personal and group development.

8

Feelings and Emotions: Fear, Guilt, Shame, Hostility, and Inadequacy

One of the most pressing questions for group members when they first enter group is "Will I be accepted?" Another question is "How shall I present myself and how much should I disclose?" Most times these questions are not asked directly but must be inferred from what is said and done by the person in sessions.

Group members are also uncertain as to which emotions or feelings can be expressed in group and the appropriate way to express what they are feeling. Leaders spend a lot of time helping members to become aware of feelings and to learn to express them appropriately. Expressions of feeling and emotion are related to questions members have about acceptance as they seek to be included and fit in. Many members feel that certain expressions lead to others making negative evaluations of them that then leads to rejection. Thus, they don't express those emotions. Others may be blocked in expression, unable to access their feelings, or may lack the words to adequately verbalize what they are experiencing.

Whatever the reason(s), leaders must be able to tune in to feelings of members, help them express them adequately and appropriately, and have access to their own inner experiencing.

Table 8.1 is an attempt to categorize levels or layers that are experienced and provide clues as to the degree of disclosing that is taking place. A discussion of feelings and emotions follows with suggestions for group experiences that focus on expressions of common feelings and emotions.

FEELINGS

What are feelings? Feelings are internal physiological reactions to your experiences (Johnson and Johnson, 1975). Emotions are "any specific feeling; any of various complex reactions with both psychical and physical manifestations, as love, hate, fear, anger, etc." (*Webster's Dictionary*, 2d Edition, 1983). Daniels and

Table 8.1
Layers and Interactions

Layers	Interactions and Self-Disclosure
Public Mask	Politeness, chitchat, little personal material exchanged.
Social/Professional	Politeness, there-and-then material, limited personal material shared.
Closeness (friends and relatives)	Here-and-now material exchanged, including feelings, confidences. Much personal material exchanged.
Intimacy	Deepest feelings shared, including some below the insulation layer.
Insulation	Prevents one from experiencing unwanted/uncomfortable feelings. Experienced as boredom, confusion, emptiness, reluctance.
Discomfort	Individual emotions and needs that are dynamic. Examples: anxiety, anger, resentment, worthlessness, helplessness, inadequacy, alienation, isolation, despair.

Horowitz (1984) consider emotions as sensitive instruments to detect that which is important in the world around us well before the rational mind recognizes what is happening (p. 20). Thus, according to them, in order to act effectively, one should develop the ability to "identify our level of arousal and then determine how we want to regulate it."

It seems reasonable to accept the notion that there are both physical and psychological reactions that comprise emotion, and feeling is the descriptive term for the physical sensation component. The psychological reaction is more difficult to describe or identify because it incorporates the psychic development of the individual which, in turn, relies on theory of development, experiences, and personality or temperament that influences responses to experiences. None of these is as capable of quantification as is feeling.

Miller, Nunnally, and Wachman (1975) describe five aspects of feeling beginning with physical sensation. Feeling begins with sensations that come through the senses of sight, hearing, touching, tasting, and smelling. The brain interprets these sensations and through this interpretation the individual decides what the "feeling" is. The interpretation is based on data received through the senses and, if the data-gathering instrument is flawed, such as sight, then that which is interpreted is subject to distortion. Feelings cause your body to respond physically so that it can become active to protect the organism. This is why the first step in feeling expression generally begins with having you focus on what your body is experiencing.

Emotions are more complex than feelings but they incorporate feelings. Interpretations given to feelings comprise some emotional content and, because of this, are unique to the individual. Emotions can be experienced as overwhelming and out of control. They can be frightening and threatening and these states activate defense mechanisms to protect the organism from experiencing these emotions. Defense mechanisms such as suppression, repression, and denial fall into this category.

Before there can be expression of feeling or emotion the individual must experience an awareness. Since feelings are an interpretation of physiological response to stimuli gathered by the senses, awareness begins with a focus on the physical. We are bombarded by sensory data and, because there is so much coming in at any one time, it may be difficult to sort it out and concentrate on any one portion.

Learning how to become more aware of what one is feeling is more than just being able to name or label the sensation. One way to teach beginning awareness is to have people focus on their bodies and report what they are aware of at that moment. For example, "I am aware of the softness of the seat and how it feels on my thighs and buttocks, the firmness of the back of the chair and how it makes my back feel supported, the tenseness in my shoulders and arms, etc." This approach also works when individuals say that they can't describe what they are feeling or that they don't know what they are feeling. The exercise at the end of this section describes a process for helping them to get in touch with what they are feeling and to name it.

Why get in touch with feelings or try to name them? One reason is that knowing what you are feeling helps you to understand the emotional reaction. Emotional reactions or emotions are defined in this discussion as the psychological component that incorporates feelings. Emotional reactions are more complex in their nature than are feelings, as they are dependent on the psychic development of the individual. Feelings tend to be more universal, such as anger, while emotions are generally unique to the individual, although they may have universal similarities, like guilt. If one can identify just what is being experienced physiologically it is easier to identify the emotional content. By identifying the emotional content one then becomes more conscious of projections, transferences, and resistances.

Another reason for focusing on feelings is that individuals can tune in better to graduations and subtleties. Learning to be aware of less intense manifestations of feelings leads to calibration of emotional response which, in turn, leads to better control. For example, learning when you are experiencing annoyance or irritation may help in lessening anger as you decide to deal with the lesser feelings so that they don't grow into the more intense feelings of anger. Becoming more aware of nuances and subtleties allows for a broader range of experiencing and responding.

It may also be that feelings must be addressed before the individual can deal with emotional reactions. The very complexity of emotional reactions may seem overwhelming to many children, and they may judge themselves incapable of dealing with something this complex. When emotional reactions are not understood or dealt with it results in splitting, repression, denial, unfinished business, and other conditions that impair the functioning of the individual. If emotional reactions can be sorted out and the various feelings identified and understood it may be easier to deal with emotional reactions.

Exercises Focusing on Feeling Awareness and Expression

- Ask group members to sit in silence, close their eyes, and concentrate on their breathing. Allow enough time for them to get comfortable and stillness to occur. Tell them to allow their breathing to become deep and even. After a period of time, 20 to 40 seconds, ask them to become aware of what their body is experiencing. Or, what are they aware of physically right now. After a minute or so have them open their eyes and tell what they were feeling. Keep the responses focused on physical experiencing. If someone has difficulty doing so, ask what they felt in different parts of the body, such as feet.

- Select a feeling that has graduations: for example, love, hate, anger, happiness. Write the graduations on the board or newsprint so that all can see them. Have the children draw a picture for each graduation, or have them tell what they feel when they experience that graduation. Doing this can make them more aware of when they experience a graduation and a discussion can provide suggestions for keeping the feeling from becoming more intense if the person wishes to do so. An example of a graduation would be comfortable, pleased, delighted, happy, ecstatic.

- Prepare a set of cards with the name of a feeling on each one. Make many more cards than there are members as you may wish to have more than one round. Turn the card over so that the

feeling is hidden and let each member select one card. They are
to act out the feeling nonverbally and see if other members can
guess the feeling. After all have had a turn discuss what was easy
to act out and what was hard. If time permits, discuss situations
where these feelings have been experienced and what it was like
for group members to have these feelings.

- Matching colors to names of feelings can be done in several
  different ways. The leader can name a feeling and let members
  select a color of crayon or felt tip and mark it on paper individu-
  ally. After several feelings have been named the colors selected
  for each can be shared and similarities and differences in perception revealed. Association for members could be discussed.
  Another procedure is for the leader to cut up strips of construction paper and let members select colors to attach to the name of
  a feeling that has been written on newsprint and posted. The same
  processing could take place.
- Another variation of matching colors to feelings is to post a
  feeling–color chart. That is, for a list of common feelings select
  a color that identifies with the feeling, such as tired—gray. Cut
  enough strips of each color for every member. At the beginning
  of each session, ask members to pick a strip that best describes
  their feeling at that time and wear it. Not only does this require
  individuals to focus on and identify what they are feeling, it also
  allows others to become aware of what others are feeling.
- Teach group members a feeling language. Many people seem
  limited in their feeling expression because they cannot think of
  words or don't know words to express what they are experiencing. Even teaching one feeling word each session can expand the
  feeling expression vocabulary.

EMOTIONS

Complex emotional reactions are often intense and many times
are frightening. They are frightening because they appear to be out
of our control, capable of destroying us and/or others. For these
reasons we may seek to repress, deny, or project them in order not
to experience them. Most are uncomfortable, like guilt, but there
can also be positive ones, like love. Another reason for not experiencing or expressing emotion may be fear of rejection by others.

That is, we fear that we will not be liked if we express certain emotions, or we have learned that we are likely to be rejected when these emotions are expressed. Our upbringing may have tried to teach control of emotions by emphasizing and reinforcing nonexpression. All of these reasons lead to constriction of emotional expressiveness.

Some of the most common emotions that many find it difficult to express or express appropriately are fear, guilt, shame, hostility, and inadequacy. Each will be defined, discussed briefly and suggested exercises presented.

Fear

Webster's Dictionary (1983) defines fear as "a feeling of anxiety and agitation caused by the presence or nearness of danger, evil, pain, etc." Some synonyms are apprehension, misgiving, timidity, trepidation, anxiety, awe, alarm, and dread. The physiological reaction to fear is to prepare to fight or flee and that is what happens when the organism feels threatened, whether the threat is real or not. Fear allows individuals to generalize potential threats from one situation to another if it is perceived to be similar in any way. Fear also causes individuals to have expectations for new situations or relationships based on what has occurred in the past. For example, a new relationship may be approached with the expectation that one will be rejected because of past experiences with rejection. Because of the fear of rejection, the individual may unconsciously sabotage the relationship and ensure that he/she is, indeed, rejected.

Although the dictionary considers fear and anxiety to be synonymous, Daniels and Horowitz (1984) quote a definition by Rowe to distinguish between fear and anxiety. They define fear as what is experienced when we know what we are afraid of, and anxiety as occurring when we are afraid and don't know what is causing us to be afraid. Rowe defines anxiety as "an unpleasant uneasiness, apprehension, uncertainty, agitation, or dread that stems from an unidentified anticipated danger" (1980, p. 44). It is more useful in this discussion to consider fear and anxiety as interrelated but not the same.

Becoming aware of fear begins with understanding that when some feelings are experienced they are less intense manifestations of underlying fear(s). For example, you may experience some bodily tension when entering the group for the first time. Your heart may beat faster and you may find that your muscles are so tense that you are uncomfortable in several parts of your body. While you may be willing to accept that you are nervous and apprehensive and rationalize that it's because of the new situation, what is probably an underlying anxiety or fear is that you will not be accepted by the group and in some way be damaged by it. This is a fear of being destroyed. However, it is also threatening in some way for you to acknowledge that you are afraid, so you suppress, repress, or deny your fears. It may also be that the fear is associated with feelings of rejection, experienced early in life, that have been transformed into anticipation of rejection when there is no rational reason for believing that you will be rejected.

A major task for the leader is to have members focus on and express the less intense manifestations of underlying fears. It may be necessary to ask directly if members are fearful about being in the group, what is fearful, and what can be done to reduce fear for them. Sometimes just being able to express that one is experiencing some form of fear helps to reduce the threat and produce more comfortable feelings.

Exercises to Reduce Fear

- A common exercise to reduce fear is systematic desensitization where individuals are put into a relaxed state and introduced to the specific fear in successive approximations. That is, they are guided through successive situations that progress from least fearful to most fearful. For more information on how to do systematic desensitization, consult *The Practice of Behavior Therapy* by Joseph Wolpe, Pergamon Press (3d edition).

- Since fear and anxiety are characterized by bodily tension, learning how to relax when faced with tension-producing situations allows individuals to maintain control and use better coping strategies. Relaxation exercises that isolate, tighten, and release muscle groups can be learned and practiced easily.

- If there are significant unresolved fears and anxieties, therapy to uncover and work through them may be indicated. This is therapy beyond the scope of that covered in this book. Individuals needing this kind of therapy should be referred.

Guilt

Guilt is defined in several ways. *Webster's Dictionary* (1983) defines it as "the feeling of having done wrong, whether real or imaginary." Perls (1969) defines it as "projected resentment" (p. 26). Jones and Banet (1976) defined guilt as anger turned inward with guilt producing feelings of depression, incompetence, help-lessness, and ultimately, self-destruction (p. 112). Alonso (1990) characterized the difference between guilt and shame by defining guilt as having the capacity of atonement and shame being per-ceived as a character flaw. Larsen (1979) feels that "guilt is really a kind of depression (often connected with anger or anxiety) resulting from some behavior or feeling of yours which you have been taught is wrong." All of the definitions have the assumption that guilt develops as a result of learning what is expected of us and failing, or feelings of failing, to live up to that expectation. What-ever the definition used, guilt is a troublesome state and can cause much psychic pain.

Strategies to deal with guilt have to begin with the individual consciously understanding just what standard or expectation has been violated or not met. Asking why someone feels guilty may not produce an answer that promotes understanding. Asking about the behavior, or nonbehavior, arouses these feelings and pursuing their antecedents may be more useful for the individual. A person may need to develop his/her own standards and expectations rather than introjecting those of others. This is a process over time that can be facilitated by discussions of standards and expectations and their payoffs. What benefits accrue to the individual who meets these standards or expectations? For example, if there is an expectation that the child will do well in school and if he/she lives up to that expectation, then the benefit is that the child will be better prepared to take care of him/herself financially when grown up. Another example would be, if the expectation of not expressing unpleasant or uncomfortable feelings is met then the benefit is that father is more accepting of the child.

There are few ways of dealing with guilt provided in the literature. Perls (1969) proposes that guilt, that is, resentment, be dealt with by exposing the conflict. In other words, when you feel guilty about not doing something, you also feel pleased and both sides need to be understood. One Gestalt exercise that is used for this purpose is "top dog, under dog." Levitsky and Perls (1970, p. 140) define top dog as roughly the equivalent of the psychoanalytic superego with shoulds, oughts, and so forth. Underdog is defined as the passively resistant part of you that makes excuses and finds reasons to delay. The two sides are asked to talk with each other. Some therapists will have the person take both sides and even change seats when speaking for one side or the other. In groups, another member can be designated to speak for one side.

Shame

Shame—"a painful emotion caused by a strong sense of guilt, embarrassment, unworthiness or disgrace" (*The American Heritage Dictionary* (1976), Houghton Mifflin Co., Boston). Closely aligned to guilt, shame arises from many of the same complex antecedents but carries the added burden of being perceived as a characteristic deeply embedded in personality, over which the individual has little or no control (Alonso, 1990). The individual is perceived by self or others as being so flawed, in this respect, that he/she can never overcome it or atone in any way. Therefore, the individual goes to great lengths to cover up and keep others from knowing the full extent of the "flaw."

Shame keeps individuals from self-examination and self-disclosure. They cannot forgive themselves for having what is perceived as a "flaw" and it, in turn, is something that cannot be mended or overcome. They resist exploring just what they are afraid is a fatal flaw and use strong defense mechanisms to hide it from others.

The group setting is ideal for presenting children with experiences that may correct misperceptions of what is shameful. By seeing others talk about themselves, similar experiences, and not be told they are "bad" or "wrong" brings about an awareness that some things perceived as shameful are not. For example, at one time people felt shamed when a child was born developmentally disabled and family members went to great lengths to keep others from knowing. Today, this is no longer considered shameful and is openly discussed. The same holds true for incest, sexual molestation, and abuse. The victims no longer need feel ashamed.

Another aspect of group that is helpful is the acceptance, warmth, and caring by the leader and members. Shame becomes less painful and easier to disclose when one feels accepted and cared for. Fostering a group climate where members feel safe encourages disclosure of shameful thoughts, behaviors, or feelings. If there are misperceptions after disclosure they can be corrected. If the individual is having difficulty sorting through these feelings, disclosure gives the group and leader an opportunity to assist, support the individual, and clarify feelings. Learning to integrate polarities and conflicting feelings is a developmental task which reduces both horizontal and vertical splitting.

Hostility

Hostile—"having or expressing enmity or opposition; antagonistic; unfriendly" (*Webster's Dictionary*). The child who exhibits hostile behaviors is easily recognized. He/she physically hurts others, verbally lashes out at others with or without provocation, acts in a brutal manner, and calls others names. Hostility is the child's reaction to deep hurts early in life, either physically, psychologically, or both. The child is seeking revenge for the pain he/she has felt.

It is difficult to have a hostile individual in a group in this setting, for it can easily polarize the group against the child and little therapeutic work will be done. The child needs individual sessions and may even need to be referred. A different group setting may be appropriate, but that setting is not covered in this book. If, however, the child exhibits one or two hostile behaviors or the hostile behaviors are not observed most of the time, he/she may benefit from the group as described herein.

Conformance to the rules of no hitting or name-calling must be enforced. These are the behaviors that should be reduced and more positive behaviors reinforced. Modeling by the leader and group members is essential. Receiving positive feedback may also contribute to modification of behavior. The leader may need to formulate a specific plan for this group member that uses strategies emphasizing desired behaviors and the resources or strengths in the group. Some suggested exercises that have the goals of reducing hostile behaviors and increasing trusting behaviors follow.

Exercises to Reduce Hostility

- Cut out lots of pictures from a magazine and/or catalog. Have enough so that each member has 10 to 12 different pictures. The pictures should be of things like trees, flowers, cars, animals, and symbols such as hearts, and so on. Provide a piece of construction paper for each member with his/her name on it.

  Direct members to select 1 or 2 pictures they associate with another member and paste them on the paper with that person's name. Then do the same for all other group members. This can be done by focusing on one member at a time, or letting group members move around to each other's paper. Every member must contribute a picture to each member. Process by having members give a reaction to the collage that emerged for them. If time permits, members can explore what the symbols or pictures mean to them. The hostile member will get positive input from other members via the pictures and is likely to give other members positive input.

- Have a go-around where each member is asked to make a positive, affirming statement about others in the group.

- Set up a role-play to demonstrate other ways of relating or resolving a conflict than by physical means.

- Teach relaxation and do a guided imagery to a place where members feel cared for. They can draw pictures or use another means of sharing their experiences in the group.

Inadequacy

Not feeling able to measure up to that which is required or feeling that one has insufficient amounts of whatever is expected or required is labeled inadequacy. It is easy to build perceptions of personal inadequacies by letting children know that they have failed to measure up to parental expectations. Not only will they feel inadequate but will likely also feel guilty. The feeling of inadequacy is persistent and carries over into adulthood.

Then too, the school setting also fosters feelings of inadequacy where children are evaluated by teachers and their peers on academic achievement, physical skills, socialization skills, and other characteristics. Whenever children face something they don't know, can't do, are criticized about or laughed at, feelings of inadequacy can ensue.

Feelings of inadequacy lead to other problems such as underachievement, perfectionistic tendencies or behaviors, and hopelessness. Underachievers set their goals lower than their abilities in order not to experience failure or feelings of inadequacy. Others fuss constantly over details so that whatever they are charged with doing is perfect and they will not be criticized and made to feel inadequate. Hopelessness is evidenced by the child not even trying, making statements that point out how stupid he/she is or agreeing with statements by others, and making put-down statements about themselves.

Children who experience feelings of inadequacy are difficult to work with in one respect: they give up easily or don't try at all. Even when they have successes they seem not to believe they are due to their ability or efforts and discount their achievements. They make all kinds of excuses in order not to try to be involved or to do something.

The child who feels inadequate, like the mildly hostile child, may benefit from being in a group. The group climate should be such that the child experiences support, encouragement, and caring for by others. The same exercises described under hostility would be useful for this member also. It is difficult to overcome feelings of inadequacy and instill a "can do" attitude. Building on successes helps to address feelings of inadequacy. Realizing that one does not have to be perfect in order to be accepted and approved of by others is also helpful.

9

Feelings and Emotions:
Anger, Depression, and Grief

It is somewhat difficult to separate these emotions and discuss them in isolation. While anger is one of the first feelings experienced, it can also be considered a complex emotion influenced and triggered by life experiences. It is also a component in depression and grief. In turn, both anger and depression are parts of grief. The following discussion may have some redundancy because of this overlapping of emotions.

In seeking to understand these intense, complex emotions the discussion will also provide descriptions of common life circumstances that give rise to them, such as divorce, death, and other kinds of separation. Examples of groups with children will also be described.

ANGER

Feelings of anger are experienced very early in life, generated by the frustration of not having needs met.

There are physiological aspects of anger as well as psychological aspects. Physical reactions to anger-producing stimuli include elevated blood pressure and accelerated heart rate. Anger's physical reaction appears to prepare the body for fight or flight. Physiological aspects are outcomes of experiences with frustrating events, such as a delay in being fed when hungry as an infant. The quality of nurturing behavior experienced as an infant and through childhood influences the intensity, frequency, duration, and causes of anger experienced and expressed.

Anger can be perceived as a reaction to a real or imaginary threat to the person's physical or psychological well-being. Not only is a threat felt, the person does not perceive him/herself as adequate to deal with the threat and therefore prepares to destroy the threat (attack) or run away (flight) by becoming angry. Because experiencing anger can be uncomfortable, overwhelming, or frightening, much time and effort are expended by individuals in denying, suppressing, repressing, or avoiding anger.

Adults who deny, suppress, repress, avoid, or act out angry feelings teach children who are under their influence and control that anger is a frightening emotion which must either be over- or under-controlled. Children tend to learn by example, and because they do, adults can help modify maladaptive ways of expressing anger by providing modeling of appropriate ways.

Anger is self-generated. Other people, situations, or events do not make us angry. We become angry because we perceive a threat to our well-being. It doesn't make much difference if the threat is real or imaginary. If it is threatening in some way, angry feelings emerge.

It is said that anger turned inward is manifested as guilt, depression, helplessness, and incompetence. Anger turned outward is manifested as violence and displacement. Helping children to recognize angry feelings, express them appropriately, and become accepting and understanding of this part of self can be facilitated in the group. However, care should be taken to screen out members who are physically abusive of others, especially if there is poor impulse control. These children need individual sessions, as they may be destructive or threatening to other group members.

Functions of Anger

Johnson (1981) describes eight functions of anger: providing energy, disrupting behavior, facilitating negative feedback, defending against vulnerability, strengthening antagonism, building awareness of threats or danger, helping to fend off opposition, and intimidating others.

Each of these functions protects the individual in some way, externalizes the threat, and prepares the body for action. People who are angry are convinced that they have been wronged by someone else in some way and are incensed at the injustice. When angry, people find it easier to express negative thoughts and feedback, lash out at the perceived threat and attack in some way. Some use anger to intimidate and control others.

The Leader and Anger

The leader should also have an understanding and acceptance of personal anger. If the leader is uncomfortable with anger, then these feelings will not be expressed or dealt with in group. The leader is then modeling that anger is not an emotion that can be expressed safely, and an opportunity to teach and model appropriate anger expression will be lost.

The first step in understanding and accepting personal anger is to become aware of when one is angry. Owning anger increases awareness of people, situations, and events that trigger angry feelings in us. This awareness allows us to analyze and calibrate the response, thus leading to more appropriate expressions. Accepting responsibility for our angry feelings prevents unwarranted blaming of others, diagnoses the perceived threat, and gives us data on which to base our response.

As many adults spend much time and effort denying, suppressing, displacing, or avoiding anger, getting in touch with angry feelings may be difficult at first. Many are fearful of the outcomes of anger expression because of past experiences of physical abuse to self or others, or other destructive and painful memories when anger was expressed. Others grew up in homes where anger was never expressed openly and/or whenever it emerged it was quickly suppressed. These adults may seek to avoid any expression of anger and/or deny having these feelings. Either way, an effective leader will work through personal responses so that he/she will model appropriate anger expression.

The leader must also become comfortable with expressions of anger by others; comfortable in the sense that he/she feels competent to adequately deal with the anger in a constructive way and seeks neither to suppress nor deny the anger, nor attack it. A major task for the group leader is to become the container for angry feelings. By holding angry feelings for members, the leader then allows them to become free to work through the feelings without being overwhelmed or threatened by the intensity of them. Allowing members to express anger and not becoming defensive does not have to be avoided, suppressed, denied, or displayed. It is also easier to teach calibration of response and awareness of less intense states such as irritation.

Appropriate Expressions of Anger

Johnson (1981) also gives some rules and guidelines for managing anger constructively. Rules include recognizing when one is angry, deciding to express the anger, developing alternatives to expression of anger, and expressing it directly when appropriate to do so.

Guidelines for appropriate expression of anger include making the expression cathartic, checking out the provocation with the other person, making the expression specific and to the person, taking responsibility for angry feelings, realizing that the intense feelings distort perceptions and responses, controlling the righteousness of one's anger, staying task-oriented, realizing the impact that anger has on the other person, and trying to express some positive feelings also.

Making the expression cathartic does not mean dumping all over the other person. After expressing a strong emotion one should feel relieved; this is the meaning of catharsis. Outbursts of strong feelings generally make the other person pay attention if expressed properly. Making "I" statements and labeling the feeling are usually sufficient.

There are times when we become angry because of our misunderstanding of what someone said, did, or meant. It is helpful to ensure that we did not misunderstand before allowing angry feelings to be expressed. It is embarrassing when we become angry only to find out that we misunderstood.

If expressing anger is appropriate then make the expression specific and direct it toward the person who is the source of that anger, not toward the group as a whole. For example, it is common in group settings when a member becomes angry that he/she will express those feelings to the group and not to the individual who did or said the provocation. When feelings are generalized then no one has to accept responsibility.

Take responsibility for your anger and realize that your perceptions may be subject to distortion because of the intense feeling. Moderate the response to be less intense than you want at this point because of potential distortion. Even if you are correct in your perceptions, a moderated response will not cost you anything and can always be upgraded, while it is almost impossible to downgrade an intense response.

When you are angry you feel that you have been done an injury or injustice that was unfair and unwarranted. There is an element of self-righteousness in anger. You are right and the other person is wrong. Stay aware of this element and try not to blame the other person. It is difficult to communicate with a self-righteous person, and all attempts to resolve the conflict or misunderstanding will fail if you remain self-righteous.

Do not wander from the issue at hand. When expressing anger, stay on topic. Don't bring in past events, feelings lingering from previous situations, anger toward others, or anything that distracts from the immediate concern.

In spite of intensity of feeling and the self-righteous component, stay in touch with the impact of your anger on the other person. If the expression of anger is resulting in increasing withdrawal or aggression of the other person, it is wise to moderate the expression or to wait until the intensity is at a level that does not promote defensiveness in the other.

Because angry feelings may be frightening, teaching methods for lessening intensity and developing control may be helpful prior to trying to work through them. Some suggestions follow.

Exercises to Deal with Anger Constructively

- Relaxation of major muscle groups will help to reduce tension and thereby lessen the body's preparation for fight or flight. Teaching members to become aware of body responses to anger and then to consciously relax those muscles helps to gain control of the feelings. Have members describe where anger is felt in their bodies, chest, stomach, gut. Get as full a description as possible of what their bodies feel like when they are angry. The triggering person, event, or situation is not important and should be saved for another time. Physical sensations are the only thing that will be addressed.

  After members have described their physical responses, have them list them or lie down with their eyes closed. Music may be played but relaxation can be taught by itself. Isolate major muscle groups one by one and have members focus on each and tighten it, then release. For example, say "Become aware of your feet. Tighten them, hold it, now, let go." Begin with the feet and move up the body.

  Instruct members to open their eyes and describe how their bodies feel and what the experience was like for them. At this point you can tell them that any time they become tense in the muscle group they have identified as their location of anger, they can relax those muscles by tensing them and then letting go. Members may need several sessions of relaxation exercises before they are able to use relaxation effectively.

- Describing anger in detail can be accomplished in several different ways: verbal reenactment, drawing an event, or role-play. Verbal reenactment occurs when a member reexperiences an anger-producing event and describes it in detail in the group setting. The leader carefully takes the members through the event by having them describe what is happening in their bodies. Where is the anger, how big is it, how heavy is it, what are the shape, color, size, intensity? Focus is not on the event, but on reexperiencing the physical sensations of anger. If the members can reexperience it, describe it in detail in the group setting, they usually find that they can control it better, and indeed, as they describe it, it becomes less intense, less threatening, and may even be disbursed.

- Group members could draw an event that produced angry feelings in them. Talking about the triggering event can help focus on triggers and suggest ways of dealing with them, or even prevent arousal of angry feelings.

- Role-play can be used much the same way as drawing. Members can describe an event, role-play both the anger and nonanger, dramatize the event with other members assuming the roles, or role-play the event with the leader taking the role of container of anger to allow the member to experiment with alternative ways of behaving in these situations.

DEPRESSION

Symptoms of Depression

Clinically depressed children should be referred, as their needs are beyond the scope of brief group counseling. Depression, in this discussion, refers to an emotional state characterized by mild symptoms of depression. In Table 9.1 the American Psychiatric Association (1986) presents the following symptoms of depression when experienced for two weeks or more. Derdeyn (1985) presents the symptoms of depression for children as interpreted from the DSM-III and the literature.

Childhood Depression

Childhood depression is influenced by many factors, but the most significant ones are life circumstances such as separation, illness, death, and divorce. Children not only face many more stressful life circumstances, but we have come to better appreciate the impact of these stressors on them. These circumstances also produce feelings of grief and both are addressed through the process

Table 9.1
Symptoms and Behavior for Depression in Adults and Children

Symptoms	Adults
changes in appetite	sleep problems
low energy, fatigue	recurrent thoughts of death, feelings of worthlessness
loss of interest in usual activities	self-reproach, excessive guilt
lessened ability to think or concentrate	
Symptoms	**Children**
decreased school performance	sleep problems
lessened socialization	low energy, fatigue
changes in appetite or weight	negative self-image
self-depreciation ideation but no sustained guilt	somatic complaints

of mourning. Therefore, the following discussion will briefly describe some life circumstances faced by children and just how group can facilitate the process of mourning.

Depression, according to Daniels and Horowitz (1984), is a statement about the individual's unexpressed and unrecognized anger. It may include self-blame, indecision, thinking that life is meaningless and futile, and a sense of worthlessness or helplessness.

In addition to life circumstances over which the child has no control and which also affect other family members, Jacobson (1971) describes another situation that may cause childhood depression, trauma or frustration in early nurturing. When early needs of the child are not met the child experiences frustration, loss, or disillusionment with the loved object. The reaction is rage, hostility, and aggression which do not do anything to gratify the unmet needs. The child then is disappointed and devalues the love object along with devaluing self and deflation of self-esteem. Children with this kind of depression are best referred.

Groups that focus on helping children access and express feelings, especially angry feelings, are useful with depression. Many will deny that they have these feelings, others will feel relief that they are at last able to openly express them, and some will have to be taught how to express these feelings.

Other approaches that help children communicate better, recognize strengths, use assertion, and learn techniques for coping, such as exercise, are also useful.

LIFE CIRCUMSTANCES THAT FOSTER DEPRESSION IN CHILDREN

Separation

There are two categories of separation, temporary and permanent. Temporary separation means that the child is separated from the other but that they will get together again. Examples of temporary separation are military service, hospitalization, and so on. Permanent separation carries the assumption that the child and the other will not be reunited. Examples of permanent separation are death and some divorces.

The kinds of temporary separation are many and the reasons varied. Children can be separated from parents because of military service, hospitalization of parents or of the child, being placed into foster care, a job that takes the parent on the road, or incarceration of a parent, for examples. Children may experience temporary separation from siblings, and this can also lead to depression and grief.

Permanent separation due to death is always difficult to deal with. It may be even more difficult when the death of a parent is unexpected and sudden. When a parent becomes ill and dies in a hospital there has usually been some time to begin to know that the illness was terminal. However, when the parent dies as a result of murder, suicide, accident, or natural disaster, there is also the crisis to contend with. There need to be differing approaches, depending on the circumstances surrounding the death and the age and level of maturity of the child.

Another permanent separation is death of a sibling. The manner of death also plays a role here just as with parents. Working with grief after a crisis is different than if there is no crisis. A major component in helping the child work through grief is the parental reaction to the sibling's death. When a child dies, parents tend to function less well and the surviving child may experience some neglect or lessened nurturing for awhile. Some parents will idealize the dead child and make unfair comparisons with the surviving child. Others will overprotect the remaining child. Some may unconsciously expect the surviving child to become the dead one and encourage him/her to assume the dead child's role and mannerisms. In some families there may be a rule of silence whereby the dead child is never mentioned. Any of these scenarios may give the surviving child an added burden to the grief he/she is already experiencing.

One circumstance of permanent separation that may be overlooked for children is when a miscarriage or stillbirth is experienced in the family. Because the child may not fully understand just what has happened and adults are working through their grief, the impact on the child may not be fully realized.

Divorce

When parents divorce, the separation of the child from one parent may be temporary or permanent. Divorce has an impact either way. Children of divorce experience depression, anxiety, anger, phobias, and guilt. They can be characterized as having realistic and unrealistic fears, lower self-esteem, lowered academic achievement, discipline problems, and health-related problems; they are tardy and absent from school more often, show increased aggressiveness and a deterioration in social interactions.

EMOTIONS ASSOCIATED WITH LOSS AND DEPRESSION

Grief

Defined as "intense mental anguish; deep remorse, acute sorrow or the like" by the *American Heritage Dictionary* (1976), grief is an emotion that is complex, having several stages and, if not resolved, continues to impact the person's life. Grief incorporates other feelings and emotions such as anger and depression and is experienced whenever there is a personal loss. The loss may be temporary but felt acutely, resulting in a kind of grief or depression. However the loss occurs, its impact is felt intensely.

Many people experience unresolved grief. Children may be particular victims because adults do not understand that they, too, need to mourn and seek to protect them from intense sorrow. Whenever this occurs there is likely to be unresolved grief.

Rando (1984) lists six forms of unresolved grief: absent, inhibited, delayed, conflicted, chronic, and unanticipated. He also defines abbreviated grief but does not consider it to be unresolved grief.

Absent grief occurs when denial is strong. The individual is stuck in stage one of grief—shock, disbelief, numbness. The person continues to function and to others it appears as if he/she is not aware that the other person is gone forever. There may even be use of the present or future tense when talking about him/her, making plans or, in some way, refusing to deal with grief.

Chronic grief is characterized by the behaviors in stage two, yearning and searching. No matter how long it has been since the loss, the person continues to long for the lost one. Adults can carry over unresolved grief from losing someone from childhood and it continues to have a negative impact on their lives.

Stage three behaviors are exhibited in inhibited grief. Unresolved, inhibited grief results in despair and disorganization. The grieving process has been interrupted and the person is stuck in this uncomfortable stage.

Conflicted grief can occur at any of the three stages. When there is both sorrow and relief at the loss and the person has difficulty accepting both feelings, there is conflict. It can also occur when the individual's feelings are in contrast to those expressed by others, *and* there is guilt or shame attached to having these differing feelings. The person is pulled between two emotions and cannot accept either one or integrate both.

Unanticipated grief can be acute. It usually happens as a result of an accident, disaster, or other unexpected circumstances. There was no preparation and the shock is immense. Elements of all three stages may be present and are experienced deeply.

Abbreviated grief appears to be short to observers; however, the person is moving through all stages because there has been time to prepare for the loss. Knowing that something is going to happen allows one to begin to understand and accept the anticipated loss. The shock, disbelief, and numbness in stage one are worked through when one first becomes aware of the illness, impending death, separation. Yearning and searching behaviors in stage two may have been resolved or at least acknowledged. The despair and disorganization of stage three may also have been reached and even though, when the actual loss occurs, there is a regression to stages one and two, the regression is brief. This allows the person to reach stage four—acceptance and reorganization—faster, all because of anticipation of the loss.

Characteristics of Unresolved Grief

There are numerous indices of unresolved grief. When several of the characteristics are observed in children after a loss, unresolved grief should be considered.

Overactivity without a sense of purpose is characteristic of some with unresolved grief. Activity for activity's sake is unproductive and used to mask uncomfortable feelings, in this case, grief. Looking at the results of activities may provide clues as to how effective the effort has been.

The child may become ill or complain of aches, pains, injuries or any ailment for which there is no physical cause. It is not uncommon for children to pick up an infection or common childhood illness, and they seem to be more susceptible when there is unresolved grief. We don't understand the mind-body connection well enough to say with confidence that the mind can cause the body to become ill. We do know that there seems to be an increase of ailments and illnesses when there has been a loss and the person is grieving. It seems to be usual and could be connected to unresolved grief.

When children's relationships with family and friends undergo a drastic change after a loss of some kind, unresolved grief could be a reason. This change may be difficult to sort out, as the changes could be due to the others' changing toward the child and he/she is only responding to them. For example, if a child loses a sibling the parents may start acting remote and aloof from the child because of their grief. The child may then internalize their behavior as his/her fault and begin to act toward them, and others, in direct contrast to his/her prior behavior. The change in behavior is not necessarily the child's unresolved grief, it is more likely the parents' unresolved grief.

There may be hostile behavior toward people associated with the loss. The child blames others for the loss and acts toward them as if they caused the loss. The child is saying "You hurt me, and I'll hurt you back." Children, as do adults, have difficulty accepting that no one was to blame for the loss and continue to seek reasons or individuals responsible.

Some children become socially withdrawn. Even those who were somewhat shy may become even more withdrawn and isolated from others. Their unresolved grief keeps them from seeking social interaction and efforts to draw them into social activities are resisted.

Children who had good grooming habits may start to exhibit poor self-care behaviors. They may be less clean, wear torn or ragged clothes, not wear clothing appropriate for the weather, omit basic articles of clothing, and so on. They may change their eating habits drastically, either overeating or undereating. All are symptomatic of unresolved grief if they have experienced a loss.

Increased tension, agitation, and insomnia are also characteristic of unresolved grief. Observations of behavior and asking questions about sleeping habits may reveal difficulties. While these are also symptomatic of mourning, if they persist, unresolved grief can be considered.

Mourning

It is difficult to determine whether unresolved grief is the issue or the person is in the process of mourning. It may be useful not to try to differentiate between the two, in most instances.

There are feelings, emotions, and physical symptoms indicative of the mourning state. When they persist over a long period, it is more difficult to resolve or work through the grief over a loss. This is one reason that working with children who experience a loss can help them work through their grief so that it does not continue to impact their lives in negative ways.

Feelings	Emotions	Physical Symptoms
emptiness	sadness	sleep problems
anger	dejectedness	eating patterns change
fatigue	depression	withdrawal from others
relief	guilt	uncomfortable dreams
	anxiety	listless, apathetic
	loneliness	crying, restless

Brenner (1984) notes that, when a parent or sibling dies, the child can be expected to take two or more years to complete the grieving process. Major components in this process for children are the age and stage of cognitive development of the child when the loss occurred, the nature of the relationship, and the quality of care received after the loss.

Lonetto (1980) proposes the following stages of cognitive conceptualization of death. From about three to five years of age children feel abandoned and want to go and get the person. They may say such things as "Let's go to heaven and get Susie." They continue to talk about the person as if he/she were alive but somewhere else.

At six to eight years old they begin to perceive death as an "entity." They like Halloween, games and stories about death as a ghost or monster, and funerals. Because they perceive death to be an entity, they also think that it can be conquered by strength or magical powers. Only those people who are too weak will be overcome by death.

By the time they are nine the ability to understand abstractions allows them to begin to know that death is final, that they too will die, and that it is a painful process.

Facilitating Mourning in Group

Derdeyn (1985) presents the following guidelines for brief interventions with children to facilitate mourning. Although his presentation focuses on individual therapy, the same guidelines can be modified for working with children in groups. The guidelines are: work through the loss, reduce impediments to mourning, and have a brief intervention with parent(s) where possible.

A group experience can facilitate working through loss, functioning either as a support group or as a therapeutic group. The goal would be to help identify and express feelings about the person and the loss of him/her. Sessions would be planned to encourage members to talk about or express in some way what they are experiencing around the loss. The leader plans and conducts the sessions to accomplish these goals and objectives but can also provide some of the reassurance proposed by Wass (1985).

Reassurance comes via three categories: providing a receptive environment, explaining or responding to implied and direct questions and statements, and verbally giving words of comfort. A receptive environment means understanding and tolerating some regressive behavior. Some children may temporarily revert to behaviors below their present maturity level. This state should be recognized, accepted, and accommodated by the leader. Another way of providing a receptive environment is to encourage members to ask questions and answer them honestly, simply, and directly. The leader must be knowledgeable and comfortable with questions around death issues and must learn how to answer them without infringing on religious and/or cultural sensitivities.

Some questions or statements will emerge indirectly and the leader should listen closely in order to respond appropriately to reassure the child. For example, in most instances of death, it was not the intent of the person to die. Even those who have been sick for a long time did not intend to abandon the child. That is the real question being asked by the child. Not, "why did they die?" But, "why did they want to leave me?" A response that reassures the child that the person did not intend to leave him/her is usually sufficient. Even in the case of suicide, leaving the child was not the intent, stopping the pain associated with living was. The unspoken question of intent may be extremely important for children who lose a parent, because they may have feelings that they were not "good" enough for the parent to want to stay with them.

Some children may ask directly or indirectly if they were to blame for the person's dying or leaving. In the cases of parental separation, divorce, or death, some children assume that they (the child) were the cause. They may say such things as, "If only I had not been bad." There is much the leader can do to help children understand that the loss was not their fault.

Verbal words of comfort can be reassuring. Telling children that they will be taken care of and loved may reassure them that they are still valued. Wass (1985) suggests telling the child that "he/she is not in danger of dying." Perhaps that statement could be modified to allow for the unknown.

Reducing impediments to mourning may be more easily accomplished in a group setting than outside the group. While members may all be mourning, it isn't shared mourning and personal pain may be better tolerated and expressed more openly if it doesn't have to incorporate the pain and distress of others sharing that loss. Even when other adults in the child's world, such as parents, help him/her to mourn, their pain and distress are felt by the child and may intensify the child's own grief, block grief, or make the child seek to take care of the adult's grief. In the group children can be helped to work through their personal grief and to give and receive support. Allowing and accepting expressions of grief that are, on the surface, selfish or negative can help the child to deal with conflicting feelings around the loss and the group may be the only place where the child would not be judged or blamed for expressing such feelings.

Having a brief meeting with parents to give information about the process of mourning and to make suggestions for helping the child can be helpful. Parents may be very aware of how grief is affecting their child but may not know what to do to help him/her through the process. Many would appreciate suggestions and the interest shown in their child. Parents, and others, can do some of the same things the group leader does but on a different level. They can reassure the child that he/she will be taken care of, that the child is not to blame for the loss; they can answer questions directly and honestly, tolerate regressive behavior, and hold and hug the child. The leader may also wish to have a list of books for the parents and for the child.

Some Ideas from the Literature

Most group activities around mourning for children in the literature emphasize expressive techniques. Many of the techniques in the literature focus on one kind of loss such as divorce or death. There are some strategies that can be adapted for losses of all kinds and the ones that are described below fall into this category. Minor modifications can allow them to be used to facilitate mourning the loss no matter what the circumstance.

McIntyre (1990) describes how to facilitate mourning by making a book about the person around whom there is a loss. The book can contain photographs and other mementoes that have meaning for the client. The purposes of the book are to review, clarify, and explore emotions around the person and the loss.

Clifford Davis (1989) uses a book of drawings for the same purposes as McIntyre. There are five parts to the book, a self-portrait that focuses on the loss. The child draws him/herself as he/she feels about the person and the loss. Also included is a description of him/herself using words. The second part is a drawing of the family in action. The third set is of faces depicting feelings with an emphasis on grieving. The fourth part is a letter written to the person wherein the child says goodby. The fifth drawing is really a redrawing of the family.

Davis (1989) also uses other techniques to aid the child in expressing and working through feelings associated with mourning a loss. They are puppets, storytelling, and clay.

Appendices

Appendix 1
Process for Review of Drawings from Fairy Tales

- Review both of the drawings together. Check off all symbols that are present in either picture. *Do not check symbols that are missing or inferred*, such as "ineffectual father" because he wasn't drawn.
- Titles and clarifications during the discussion period *are* appropriate to use in the checklist.
- Refer to the list of existential issues and developmental issues. For individuals count the number of symbols in each category. Do the same for the group.
- Whenever possible, have more than one person review the drawings using the checklist. Compile agreement and frequency of checks.

Appendix 2
Categorization of Symbols

Symbol in Fairy Tale	Existential Issue
Left in the forest	Aloneness
Acquiring treasure	Achieving higher humanity
Crossing water	Successful transition to a higher plane
Bird on roof, duck on water	Superior benevolent power
Returning home safely	Establishing human relationships
Bringing treasure home	Assuming responsibility
Symbol	**Developmental Issue**
Bread crumbs on path	Failure to meet safety needs
Stones on path	Meeting safety needs
Gingerbread house	Attractiveness of giving in to oral greediness
Eating the gingerbread house	Destructive oral desires
Witch	Evil, destructive aspects of personality
Killing the witch	Controlling the evil, destructive aspects of personality
Tricking the witch to climb in oven; substitution of bone for finger	Goal directed behavior versus instinctual impulses or wish fulfilling fantasies
Crossing the pond separately on the duck	Individuation

References

Agazarian, Yvonne (1992). Contemporary theories of group psychotherapy: A systems approach to the group-as-a-whole. *International Journal of Group Psychotherapy, 42* (2):177–204.

Alonso, Ann (1990). *Shame and restoration of self-esteem in the group.* Presentation at the Mid-Atlantic Group Psychotherapy Society Conference. Baltimore, MD.

American Heritage Dictionary (1976). Boston, MA: Houghton Mifflin Co.

American Psychiatric Association (1986). *Diagnostic and statistical manual of mental disorders* (3d ed.). Washington, DC: American Psychiatric Association.

Belcher, V. B. (1983). History need not repeat itself: Make children aware of child abuse through literature. *The School Counselor* (September):44–47.

Berman, Leon (1991). A dream of the red shoes: Separation confict in the phallic-narcissistic phase. *Journal of Psychoanalysis 72* (2):233–42.

Bettelheim, Bruno (1975). *The uses of enchantment.* New York: Vintage Books.

Brenner, Avis (1984). *Helping children cope with stress.* Lexington, MA: Lexington Books.

Campbell, Joseph (1988). *The power of myth-with Bill Moyers* (Betty Sue Flowers, ed.). New York: Doubleday.

Carkuff, R. R., and B. G. Berenson (1977). *Beyond counseling and therapy* (2d ed.). New York: Holt, Rinehart & Winston.

Cashdan, Sheldon (1988). *Object relations therapy*. New York: W. W. Norton.

Cohene, Susan, and Lee S. Cohene (1989). Art therapy and writing with deaf children. *Journal of Independent Social Work, 4*:21–46.

Corey, Gerald (1990). *Theory and practice of group counseling*. Monterey, CA: Brooks/Cole.

Crain, William C. (1983). The impact of hearing a fairy tale on children's immediate behavior. *Journal of Genetic Psychology, 143* (1) (September):9–17.

Daniels, Victor, and Laurence Horowitz (1984). *Being and caring* (2d ed.). Palo Alto, CA: Mayfield Publishing Co.

Davies, Evan (1988). Reframing, metaphor, myths and fairy tales. *Journal of Family Therapy, 10* (1) (February):83–92.

Davis, Clifford (1989). The use of art therapy and group process with grieving children. *Issues in Comprehensive Pediatric Nursing, 12*:269–80.

Derdeyn, Andre (1985). "Childhood," in *Depressive states and their treatment* (Vamik Volkan, ed.). Northvale, NJ: Jason Aronson, Inc.

Dunne, Pam B. (1988). Drama therapy techniques in one-to-one treatment with disturbed children and adolescents. *Arts in Psychotherapy, 15*:139–49.

Ellis, Albert (1992). Group rational-emotive and cognitive-behavioral therapy. *International Journal of Group Psychotherapy, 42* (1):63–80.

Ferrara, Nadia (1991). Luke's map of the journey: Art therapy with a Cree Indian boy. *Journal of Child and Youth Care, 6* (3):73–78.

Fromm, Eric (1956). *The art of loving*. Perennial Library. New York: Harper & Row.

Ganzarain, Ramon (1992). Introduction to object relations group psychotherapy. *International Journal of Group Psychotherapy, 42* (2):205–23.

Gazda, George (1989). *Group Counseling* (4th ed.). Boston, MA: Allyn and Bacon.

Heuscher, Julius (1989). Dread and authenticity. *The American Journal of Psychoanalysis, 49* (2):139–57.

Hill, Laura (1992). Fairy tales: Visions for problem resolution in eating disorders. *Journal of Counseling and Development, 70* (5) (May-June):584–87.

Huddleston, Roz (1989). Drama with elderly people. *British Journal of Occupational Therapy, 52* (8) (August):298–300.

Jacobson, Edith (1971). *Depression: comparative study of normal, neurotic and psychotic conditions.* New York: International Universities Press.

Jessness, Carl (1962). *The Jessness inventory.* Palo Alto, CA: Consulting Psychologists Press.

Johnson, David (1981). *Reaching out* (2d ed.). Englewood Cliffs, NJ: Prentice-Hall.

Johnson, D. W., and F. Johnson (1975). *Joining together: Group theory and group skills.* Englewood Cliffs, NJ: Prentice-Hall.

Jones, John E., and Anthony Banet (1976). "Dealing with anger," in *The 1976 annual handbook for group facilitators.* La Jolla, CA: University Associates.

Katz, Susan (1987). Photocollage as a therapeutic modality for working with groups. *Social Work with Groups, 10* (4):83–90.

Kernberg, Otto (1990). *Borderline and pathological narcissism.* Northvale, NJ: Jason Aronson, Inc.

Klein, Melanie (1975). "Mourning and its relation to manic-depressive states," in *Love, guilt and reparation,* and other works. New York: Dell.

Klingman, Arrigdor, Elinore Koenigsfeld, and Dafna Markman (1987). Art activity with children following a disaster: A preventive-oriented crisis intervention modality. *The Arts in Psychotherapy, 14*:153–66.

Kohut, H. (1971). *The analysis of the self.* New York: International Universities Press.

———(1977). *The restoration of the self.* New York: International Universities Press.

Larsen, Tony (1979). *Trust yourself.* San Luis Obispo, Calif. Impact Publishers.

Lehmkuhl, Ulrike (1988). From "Hans in luck" to "Superman": The importance of fairy tales in psychotherapy with children. *Acta Paedopsychiatrica, 51* (1):28–37.

Levitsky, Abraham, and Fritz Perls (1970). "The rules and games of gestalt therapy," in *Gestalt therapy now* (Joen Fagan and Irma Lee Shepherd, eds.). New York: Harper Colophon Books.

Lonetto, R. (1980). *Children's conceptions of death*. New York: Springer Publishing Co.

Mahler, Margaret (1968). *On human symbiosis and the vicissitudes of individuation*. New York: International Universities Press.

McIntyre, Barbara (1990). Art therapy with bereaved youth. *Journal of Palliative Care, 6* (1):16–23.

Miller, Sherod, Elam W. Nunnally, and Daniel B. Wachman (1975). *Alive and aware*. Minneapolis, MI: Interpersonal Communication Programs, Inc.

Mosley, Jenny (1988). Dramatherapy: Helping children with behavior problems. *Maladjustment and Therapeutic Education, 6* (2):120–26.

———— (1991). An evaluative account of the working of a dramatherapy peer support group within a comprehensive school. *Support for Learning, 6* (4):156–64.

Perls, Fritz (1969). *Gestalt therapy verbatim*. Moab, Utah: Real People Press.

Radomisli, Michael (1981). Stereotypes, stepmothers and splitting. *The American Journal of Psychoanalysis, 41* (2):121–27.

Rando, T. A. (1984). *Grief, death and dying*. Champaign, IL: Research Press.

Robbins, Arthur (1980). "Introduction to expressive therapy," in *Expressive therapy*, (Robbins and Contributors). New York: Human Sciences Press.

Rogers, Carl (1975). Empathic: An unappreciated way of being. *The Consulting Psychologist, 5* (2):2–9.

Rowe, C. J. (1980). An outline of psychiatry. Dubuque, ILL. William C. Brown.

Ryerson, Margaret (1977). Death education and counseling for children. *Elementary School Guidance and Counseling, 11* (3):165–74.

Schapiro, Edward (1968). The psychodynamics and developmental psychology of the borderline patient: A review of the literature. *The American Journal of Psychoanalysis, 135* (11):1305–13.

Scheidlinger, Saul (1985). Group treatment of adolescents: An overview. *American Journal of Orthopsychiatry, 55* (1):102–11.

Sourkes, Barbara (1991). Truth to life: Art therapy with pediatric oncology patients and their siblings. *Journal of Psychosocial Oncology, 9* (2):81–96.

St. Clair, Michael (1986). *Object relations and self-psychology*. Monterey, CA: Brooks/Cole.

Thiessen, Irmgard (1985). A new approach with fairy tales as metaphors and anchoring devices in hypnotherapy. *Medical Hypoanalysis*, 6 (1–2) (January-April):21–26.

——— (1988). *The importance of metaphors in fairy tales in promoting ego strength values and well being.* Presented at the annual meeting of the International Council of Psychologists in Singapore.

Walker, Virginia, and Mary Lunz (1976). Symbols, fairy tales and school age children. *The Elementary School Journal, 77* (2):94–100.

Wass, H. (1985). Helping young children cope with the death of a parent. *Thanatos, 10,* 5–7.

Webster's Dictionary (2d ed.) (1983). New York: Dorset & Baber.

Wolpe, Joseph (1982). *The practice of behavior therapy* (3d ed.). New York: Pergamon Press.

Yalom, Irvin (1985). *The theory and practice of group psychotherapy* (3d ed.). New York: Basic Books.

Index

About the Author

NINA W. BROWN has taught counseling at Old Dominion University in Virginia since 1968. She is the author of *Teaching Group Dynamics: Process and Practices* (Praeger, 1992).

DATE DUE